COLORS OF CALIFORNIA
AGRICULTURE

ALFALFA FLOWER	ALMOND TREE GROVE	AMARANTH	ARKANSAS BLACK APPLE	ARTICHOKE	ASIAN PEAR	ASPARAGUS	BEAN FIELD	BING CHERRY	BLACK BEAN
BLACK BULL	BLACK EYED PEA	BLACK FIG	BLACKBERRY	BLOOD ORANGE	BLUEBERRY	BOK CHOY	BROCCOLI CROWN	BROCCOLI FLOWER	BROWN TURKEY FIG
BRUNETTE BEAUTY DATE	BRUSSELS SPROUTS	BURNT PRAIRIE	BUTTER LETTUCE	CABBAGE FIELD	CADENERA SWEET ORANGE	CARA CARA ORANGE	CARROT	CELERY	CHANDLER GRAPEFRUIT
CHILI PEPPER	CHINESE EGGPLANT	CILANTRO	CLEMENTINE FINA ORANGE	CLING PEACH	COLLARD GREEN	COMPOST PILE	CORN STALK	COTTON BALE	COTTON BLOSSOM
CUCUMBER	DAIRY COW	DAIRY FEED	EGG SHELL	FARM WORKER DENIM	FARM WORKER HAT	FAUX PLASTIC GRAPE	FENNEL FIELD	FIG LEAF	FINGERED CITRON (BUDDHA'S HAND)
FLAME GRAPEFRUIT	FREE RANGE FRYER	FRENCH PLUM	FUKUMOTO NAVEL ORANGE	GOAT	GOLF COURSE	GOPHINATOR	GRAFTED GRAPEVINE	GRAIN PILE	GRAZING LAND
GREEN APPLE	GREEN BELL PEPPER	GREEN OLIVE	GREEN TOMATO	HARVESTED SUDAN FIELD	HAAS AVOCADO	HAY	HONEYDEW MELON 01	HONEYDEW MELON 02	HORSERADISH LEAF
HORSERADISH ROOT	IRRIGATION WATER 01	IRRIGATION WATER 02	IRRIGATION WATER 03	JOHN DEERE TRACTOR	KALE	KIWI	KOHLRABI	KUMQUAT	LATEX GLOVE

LEEKS	LEMON	LOQUAT	MANDARINQUAT	MARIJUANA	MARY ELLEN SWEET LIME	MEDICAL MARIJUANA	MELLOW GOLD GRAPEFRUIT	MICHAL MANDARIN ORANGE	MILLSWEET LEMON
MONTEREY MUSHROOM	MORO BLOOD ORANGE	NEW HOLLAND TRACTOR	NOPAL	NOPAL FRUIT	OLD GROWTH GRAPEFRUIT	ONION	ORANGE	ORGANIC DRIED HACHIYA PERSIMMON	ORGANIC GARLIC
ORGANIC PURPLE CAULIFLOWER	OROBLANCO GFT HYBRID WHITE GRAPEFRUIT	OYSTER	PACKING BOX	PALM TREE	PAVED FARM ROAD	PEACH	PERSIMMON	PESTICIDE LATEX GLOVE	PETERBILT DUMP TRUCK
PINOIT NOIR	PISTACHIO	POMEGRANATE	PORTABLE TOILET	POULTRY SHED	PUMMELO X RUBY NUMBER 1	PUMPKIN	RADISH	RAINIER CHERRY	RAISIN GRAPE
RASPBERRY	RED APPLE	RED BELL PEPPER	RED CHARD	RED LETTUCE	RED ONION	RED TRUCK	RED VALENCIA ORANGE	RICE FIELD	RIPENING PEAR
ROMA TOMATO	RUBIDOUX PUMMELO	SAFFLOWER 01	SAFFLOWER 02	SCIABICA'S UNFILTERED EXTRA VIRGIN OLIVE OIL	SHEEP WOOL	SILAGE	SPINACH FIELD	STRAWBERRY	SUDAN GRASS
SUGARBEET FIELD	SULFUR	SUNFLOWER	SWEET ALYSSUM	SWEET POTATO	TAHITIAN PUMMELO	TANGO MANDARIN	THOMPSON SEEDLESS GRAPE	THORNLESS MEXICAN LIME	TIN FARM BUILDING
TRAY OLIVE	TRELLIS	VALENCIA ORANGE	VANIGLIA SANGUIGNO ORANGE	WALNUT GROVE	WHITE POTATO	WORKER HOUSING	YELLOW BELL PEPPER	YELLOW CHARD	ZUCCHINI BLOSSOM

COLORS OF CALIFORNIA AGRICULTURE

BY PETER GOIN AND PAUL F. STARRS

NUMBER SIXTY-TWO

IN A SERIES OF KEEPSAKES ISSUED FOR ITS MEMBERS BY THE FRIENDS OF THE BANCROFT LIBRARY

THIS IS NUMBER _413_ OF THE 2018 BANCROFT KEEPSAKE

THE BANCROFT LIBRARY

UNIVERSITY OF CALIFORNIA

BERKELEY 2018

Library of Congress Cataloguing in Publication Data

Goin, Peter, 1951—
Starrs, Paul F., 1957—

Colors of California Agriculture / Peter Goin and Paul F. Starrs

ISBN 978-1-893663-48-0 (13 digit); 1-893663-48-5 (10 digit) (hardcover : alk. paper)

1. Agriculture—History and Contemporary. 2. Photography—Practice and Theory. 3. California—Landscape and Economy. 4. The Bancroft Library—University of California. 5. Geography and Landscape Studies.

Library of Congress Control Number: 2018943511

Cover Art: Peter Goin; plus frontispiece Colors of California Agriculture: From Alfalfa flower to Zucchini blossom
The front cover top left square is Alfalfa flower; bottom right, Latex Glove. The back cover top left square is Leeks; bottom right, Zucchini Blossom.
Cover & Interior Design/Typesetting: Dawn M. McCusker of Harrisonburg, Virginia.

Colors of California Agriculture is published by The Bancroft Library, University of California, Berkeley. A "Keepsake" version went solely to members of the Friends of The Bancroft Library in 2018.

Orders, inquiries, and correspondence should be addressed to:
Black Rock Institute
P.O. Box 14430
Reno NV 89507
http://blackrockinstitute.org

Printed in China through Four Colour Print Group, Louisville, Kentucky
First Edition, 2018
The paper used in this publication meets the minimum requirements of ANXI/NISO Z39.48—1992 (R 1997) (Permanence of Paper)

CONTENTS

DIRECTOR'S SALUTE

ELAINE C. TENNANT

JAMES D. HART DIRECTOR, THE BANCROFT LIBRARY

In 2011 Peter Goin and Paul F. Starrs donated to The Bancroft Library the archive they created in producing their *Field Guide to California Agriculture* (Berkeley: University of California Press, 2010). Included were research materials of various kinds, drafts, a portfolio of exquisite large format exhibition prints, and hundreds of smaller prints and digital reference proofs. This remarkable collection, the *Peter Goin and Paul F. Starrs California Agriculture Archive*, is the work of a couple of Western visionaries whose contemporary archive engages, expands, and redefines aspects of Hubert Howe Bancroft's original vision and mission. The collection that HHB built has played a supporting role in several recent Goin and Starrs projects on California agriculture—their *Field Guide* in 2010 and Bancroft Gallery Exhibition, *The Colors of California Agriculture* in 2013, curated with Jack von Euw—and now this volume in which they marry their hard work from the *Field Guide* with historical artifacts from Bancroft's agricultural collections. In doing so they help the Bancroft collection fulfil its intended mission—to provide the data to support the writing of successive of histories of the West, its peoples, and their activities.

In 1890, looking back over more than thirty years of his career as a businessman, collector, interviewer, and historian, Hubert Howe Bancroft recalled in his autobiography, *Literary Industries*, both his vision of the American West and the purpose of the collection he assembled to document and serve it.

[…] I cannot but feel that I was but the humble instrument of some power mightier than I, call it providence, fate, environment, or what you will. That I should leave my home and friends at the east and come to this coast an unsophisticated boy, having in hand and mind the great purpose of securing to a series of commonwealths, destined to be second in intelligence and importance to none the sun has ever shone upon, more full and complete early historical data than any government or people on earth enjoy to-day, is not for a moment to be regarded as the facts in the case. It was the vital expression of a compelling energy. (Bancroft 2013, 2–3)

The notions of American exceptionalism and manifest destiny that hover around Bancroft's exuberant mission statement may sound dated or a little bombastic now, but his ambitious goal of securing for future generations the full and complete historical record of this place, and the ecumenical reach of his collecting were nothing short of visionary. Because history itself was his passion and became his occupation and business (he named his firm "The History Company"), no category of evidence, format of documentation, subject or social group was irrelevant or ineligible for his collection, so long as it related to the West. As a result, he collected materials that many libraries did not, and these unique sources enable research that cannot be conducted elsewhere. HHB's breadth of focus, enthusiasm for everything, and emphasis on data as the raw material of history writing make the collection he founded endlessly useful for the many communities and "commonwealths" that call this region home and the thousands of researchers who seek and continue to find information to support their inquiries at Bancroft.

In *Colors of California Agriculture*, Paul Starrs and Peter Goin pair historical materials from Bancroft agricultural collections, some reaching back into the mid-nineteenth century, with Peter's recent photographs of agriculture in California. In Paul's descriptions of these then-and-now juxtapositions, the Bancroft historical witnesses to California's agricultural past serve as touchstones for questions suggested by Peter's images. The merry earnestness of the Goin photographs presented with their specific historical counterparts and the Starrs descriptions of both are an invitation to gasp at the beauty and diversity of the agricultural bounty of the state, to laugh out loud at some visual jokes, and to think hard about the next hundred years of agriculture in California. This is a densely illustrated album to thumb through at random, a quick review of recent developments in California agriculture, and a gentle catalyst for serious discussion of issues confronting the pastures of plenty—all viewed in the context of the history of California agriculture to this point and filled with quotable data. Or maybe it's truly a primer or a source book. Open it to any page. Listen to a modern color photograph talk to the historical one next to it. Read the captions, rich in insider details. See change. Tell the story.

The University Chronicle of 1905–06 includes a report to the UC President and Regents by Reuben G. Thwaites dated 14 October, describing the priceless content and monetary value of the Bancroft Collection. Thwaites, Superintendent of the Wisconsin Historical Library, was commissioned to do the appraisal, which concludes: "The Bancroft Library may […] at once enter the field of historical publication, with results highly creditable to the University. […] The opportunity for scholarly work in this direction is, both in freshness and breadth, quite unexampled elsewhere in America." The University of California purchased the Bancroft collection the following month. The same volume of the *Chronicle* includes a piece entitled "What a University Farm Is For" by Liberty Hyde Bailey of the Cornell University College of Agriculture. Bailey argued strongly for the inclusion of an agricultural school within the university as a laboratory teaching facility. In 1907 the University of California purchased the Jerome Davis farm, which eventually became UC Davis. Several of the historical photographs included in this volume date from that period in University of California history and are held at The Bancroft Library, where they have been waiting for more than a century to help Peter and Paul present this exceptional look at the history of California agriculture.

CALIFORNIA'S FINEST

JACK VON EUW, *CURATOR*

There is nothing in the intellect that was not first in the senses

The Peripatetic Axiom, Thomas Aquinas,

De veritate (after Aristotle) (1256–1259 AD)

When the "Saints" Peter and Paul, respectively Messrs. Goin and Starrs, came marching in to The Bancroft Library in 2006, the topic of California Agriculture—let alone the "colors" thereof—seldom if ever arose in my conversations. Mining or logging seemed closer to my field of vision than Bob Dylan's "ploughmen dig my earth…" Images that spoke to me of agriculture in California came from Steinbeck books read long ago, Dorothea Lange's photographs for the Farm Security Administration, and from work by Ted Streshinsky documenting the birth of the United Farm Workers in Delano. That's a sad lacuna in my education given that in 2018 the Berkeley campus is celebrating the sesquicentennial of the "Organic Act," the 1868 document that founded the University of California as a land-grant institution of higher learning, dedicated in particular to providing the state with agronomists, metallurgists, land managers, and lawyers. One has only to glance up at the decorative elements— sheaves of wheat and other grains—that adorn South Hall, the oldest building on the Berkeley campus, to realize

what a significant role agriculture has played not only in the establishment of the University, but also in cutting edge research into a host of issues vital to the production of crops, animal husbandry, and the sensible stewardship of California's natural resources. Another major indicator of the importance of agriculture for the University is Giannini Hall. In 1928, Bancitaly Corporation endowed the Giannini Foundation of Agriculture Economics in memory of Amadeo P. Giannini, founder of San Francisco's Bank of Italy, which subsequently morphed into the Bank of America.

I am, I suppose, a stereotypical northern California coastal urbanite, a traipser along asphalt and pavement who appreciates tree-lined streets, patches of green that dot the Berkeley campus and the town, and views of San Francisco Bay where the ocean shimmers seductively beyond the Golden Gate. My closest brushes with agriculture are at the Downtown Berkeley farmers market where it is Judy, my wife, who chooses and I carry. Where vegetables are concerned Judy has a promiscuous streak; she loves them one and all. Spring greens are especially irresistible. Tender fava beans appear and disappear in the time it takes to shell the first or second batch scored from the market and toted home as precious cargo in recycled bags. Young garlic, here today and gone tomorrow, its cloves hardly formed, makes the best delicately pungent aioli. Summertime and the "living is easy" on the California Coast, when sweet red Gypsy peppers are ready to blacken on hot coals, the scent of melons with mellifluous monikers like Sharlyn, Galia, and Casaba perfumes the market air, and when we gorge on the taste and texture of heirloom tomatoes well into September. "Locally sourced and seasonally grown" was all I ever needed to know. Living at the home place for California Cuisine, and just a few blocks from Alice Waters' Edible Schoolyard, it's true that if you are able and willing to pay the price you can eat seasonally and freshly the whole year round.

Stepping down from the top rung of the food chain, is to realize the implausibility of farmers markets feeding and sustaining the entire state of California, never mind the nation, and still have surplus for export to distant shores. The larger growers and purveyors of organics may supply North Berkeley's cramped and marvelous Monterey Market and Berkeley Bowl, last resorts for Berkeley Foodies, but not the ubiquitous supermarket chains and fast food venues of mass consumption. This is where California Big Ag comes in. How else to grow all the tomatoes for catsup because Heinz is not about to process organic heirlooms to make paste?

That day in 2006 when I first met Peter and Paul was a game changer and a boon for Bancroft. They came as two wise men bearing the promise of future gifts, a box of eye-opening photographs, and a generous proposal to donate what would eventually become the *Peter Goin and Paul F. Starrs California Agriculture Archive*. The two of them cultivated my understanding—early on narrow to the point of hypoxemia—of the vital significance of the agricultural bounty that is California.

Now in 2018, I hold a stubby book in my hand, the *Field Guide to California Agriculture*, a weighty publication in every sense of the word, consisting of 475 pages, brimming with information presented in the form of Paul Starrs' voluble text, colorful graphics, and a suite of stunning photographs by Peter Goin. The paperback edition is surely meant to fit in a backpack or on the front passenger seat or the glove box of your car once you decide to get rid of all the maps you rarely use anymore. The book is a mini-encyclopedia intended to be within easy reach and readily consulted at the highway rest stop. At least that's what I did the last time Judy and I drove to Los Angeles on Interstate 5 from Berkeley. Once the Bay Area, the redwoods, and a cool ocean breeze are left behind, it becomes evident that there is a lot more than meets the eye, even in an air-conditioned pod motoring toward the Southland.

Strawberry Fields, Plastic Covers for Fumigation, UC Agricultural Extension, Salinas Valley,
Ansel Adams, 1966. Gelatin silver print, The Fiat Lux Photograph Collection, University Archives.
The Bancroft Library, University of California Berkeley, BANC UARC PIC 1800:276

Spraying Lettuce Field, Monterey County, 2007, Peter Goin.

What is there to see? Trucks loaded with mountains of green or red tomatoes rumble past, leaving our little station wagon vibrating in their wake, a signal that Dorothy is not in Berkeley anymore. Acre after rectangular acre, row upon evenly spaced green row next to great swaths of seemingly barren brown fields; tall aluminum arms spouting long arcing sprays of water circle slowly like whales mounted on carousels; gleaming white in the blazing sunlight, long and low horizontal structures when glimpsed from the highway appear like temples in the hazy distance—as if Amy Semple McPherson had returned to hold one last mega revival—and still miles away the sweet and sour stench wafts up, more acrid by the second, anticipating our arrival at that dense-packed bovine city called Harris Ranch. That's when the *Field Guide* replete with clear descriptions and vivid visuals of greenhouses, fields of soybeans, spinach, and asparagus rescues me from drowning in my own urban ignorance.

The title of this Keepsake derives from an eponymous exhibition, *The Colors of California Agriculture*, held in The Bancroft Library Gallery from April 26th through July 26th, 2013, which in turn is the abbreviated title of one of Peter Goin's mural-sized digital prints called, "The Colors of California Agriculture: From Alfalfa Flower to Zucchini Blossom." The print consists of a Bauhaus-like grid of 160 individual color squares, each an essential distillation of the dominant color of an agricultural object both organic and non-organic. This Josef Albers on steroids mural represents the diversity of agricultural products produced in California and the variety of implements and machinery used in their cultivation. Grids with precisely planted equidistant rows are necessary to accommodate the machines needed for industrial scale crop management. As Paul Starrs elucidates in more detail elsewhere, the University of California from its earliest years, first at Berkeley, then Davis and Riverside, contributed to the development of innumerable innovations

and techniques that made industrial farming possible. These innovations, financed by partnerships and collaborations with business, encompassed more than the mechanics and machinery of farming—although there are many such examples. They include the breeding and husbandry of various strains of vegetables and fruits designed by University scientists to withstand the vicissitudes of Mother Nature and the rigors of transportation. The development of the "square tomato" with its tough skin, uniform shape and size is ideal for mechanical harvesting, shipping to the plants that manufacture catsup made from tomato product pumped from gleaming tanks trucked on eighteen wheelers. UC engineers had a hand in devising the irrigation technology that made Salinas and Monterey County the lettuce capital of the world.

Beginning in 1949 the Friends of The Bancroft Library issued a yearly Keepsake for its members. The topics have encompassed the 1848 treaties with Mexico (number 1), overland journeys to the Pacific (number 15), nine classic California photographers (number 23), and latest but not least *Colors of California Agriculture* (number 62). This keepsake has taken time to come to fruition—nearly ten years have elapsed since we first discussed the idea of a publication, and five years since the exhibition. I hope when the members of the Friends receive this beautifully produced publication they will be delighted and consider the cornucopia of information and images presented between the covers worth waiting for.

HOLDINGS AT THE BANCROFT LIBRARY

Walking down Campanile Way, banners affixed to lampposts extol "Berkeley's 150 Years of Light." The fact is The Bancroft Library holdings documenting the history of agriculture, land use, and ownership precede the founding of the University by at least 100 years. The Library holdings reflect the history

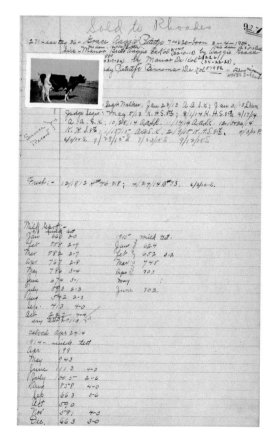

Record of Grace Aaggie Pietertje, # 271, Otis H. Lockhart. Otis Hw. Lockhart records: Los Angeles, Calif.

BANC MSS 2010/192

A Birds-eye View on the Cattle Ranch of Daniel McCarty. Thompson & West. Print on paper: lithograph; Robert B. Honeyman, Jr. Collection of Early Californian and Western American Pictorial Material.

BANC PIC 1963.002:0483:02—B

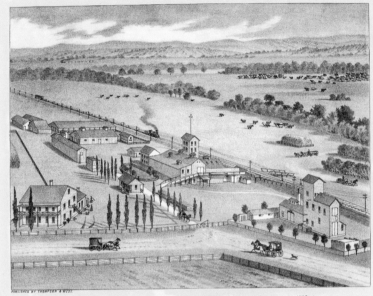

A BIRDS-EYE VIEW ON THE CATTLE RANCH OF **DANIEL MC CARTY,** 352 ACRES, PURCHASED IN 1878, ALONG THE AMERICAN RIVER 1½ MILE EAST OF SACRAMENTO, CAL.

of agriculture and land ownership in California and the University's contributions to it in a variety of ways, beginning with its collection of *diseños*, the hand drawn maps that hopefully but vaguely delineated the borders of enormous tracts of ranchos when California belonged to Spain (1769–1821) and Mexico (1822–1846). The *Miller & Lux Records* (BANC MSS C-G 163), comprising more than 1,000 linear feet, is certainly one of the most voluminous and important primary sources on agriculture in Bancroft, which has fueled at least multiple dissertations and at least two books. Consisting primarily of correspondence, business, and legal records, the archive documents the operations of one of the largest agricultural and land holding conglomerates in California. Charles Lux and Henry Miller were German immigrants, trained as butchers, who started out supplying

the burgeoning city of San Francisco with meat. By the time Henry Miller died in 1916, government estimates listed his land holdings as 1,400,000 acres, although the actual amount of land he controlled through lease and grazing rights was likely far larger. The records show that "Big Ag" was a major force in California long before there was a name for it.

There are two linked collections on agriculture in The Bancroft of special interest: The *Paul Shuster Taylor Papers* (BANC MSS 84/38 c) and The *Farm Security Administration Photograph Collection* (BANC PIC 1942.008). These collections are linked because the FSA photographs were part of the *Ralph W. Hollenberg Collection of Materials Relating to the Farm Security Administration, Region IX*, bulk dates 1938–1945 (BANC MSS C-R 1), which came to

Bancroft via Paul Taylor who was a professor of economics at Berkeley from 1922–1962. His research methodology was at a far remove from that of his colleagues and theorists of the "dismal science," employing fieldwork practices from ethnography, folklore, and sociology, rather than descriptive quantitative economics. Taylor's primary research concerned rural populations and their relationship to the land, and he relied on acute observation and meticulous recording of what his subjects told him in the field. Taylor's contribution to the study of economics was both intellectual—his research provided him with means to predict trends—and practical, as Taylor fearlessly entered into the arena of public policy.

In my view, Paul Taylor exhibited an uncanny prescience in hiring Dorothea Lange, whom he married some years later, though as a "typist" because the Resettlement Agency bureaucracy as yet had no category for photographer. Lange, one of the greatest photographers of the twentieth century, channeled Taylor's methodical observations into indelible visual documents that transcended their documentary function and ascended into the pantheon of artistic masterpieces. When the Farm Security Administration took over the Resettlement Agency it created the FSA Information Division, under the direction of Roy Stryker. As photography became an increasingly important part of the government's New Deal narrative, Stryker employed a cadre of photographers, including such future luminaries as Walker Evans, Dorothea Lange, Russell Lee, Gordon Parks, Marion Post Wolcott, Arthur Rothstein, Ben Shahn, John Vachon, and Marjory Collins. *The Farm Security Administration Photograph Collection* in Bancroft features an exceptionally large number of Lange photographs because many of Lange's assignments were in California, which Region IX represented along with Nevada, Arizona, and Utah.

Strawberry Fields, Plastic Covers for Fumigation

Ansel Adams's rendition is pure theater, a stage set with a dramatically dark sky that forms the distant horizon. The rows of plastic are seemingly touched by a divine light and transmogrified into a graphic tour de force of one point perspective. Like a Moses, Adams came down from the High Sierra and gave his tribe of photographers the Ten Commandments of the Zone System. Adams along with Edward Weston, Imogen Cunningham, and other members of the f/64 Group established the West Coast tradition of the "straight" modernist, pre-visualized, and exquisitely executed fine print. According to the tenets of the Zone System, a fine and artistically worthy gelatin silver print demanded maximum depth of field and the widest tonal variation possible, from deepest shadow to brilliant highlights. Adams was known for his powerfully compelling and reverential photographs of Yosemite in particular and California's Sierra Nevada in general. He became, through a popular series of technical books and the dissemination of his photographs, the embodiment of the rugged outdoorsman in the West and arguably the most admired photographer in America when UC President Clark Kerr asked him to photograph the entirety of the University of California System in 1963. Taking almost four years to complete, the aim of the project was to publish a handsome coffee-table book by 1968 to commemorate the centennial of the founding of the University. In addition to the book, the project produced the 601 prints in the University Archives in Bancroft. Although I admire the beauty and the mystery of Adams's photograph of the Strawberry Fields, I do wonder how much his interpretation informs us about the ostensible subject matter? Clark Kerr's commission took Ansel Adams out of Yosemite, but Kerr could not take Yosemite out of Adams.

Spraying Lettuce Field, Monterey County

The visions of precisely planted rows featured in Peter Goin's photograph, *Spraying Lettuce Field...* and in Ansel Adams's of *Strawberry Fields [in the ...] Salinas Valley* could not be more different—color versus black and white, digital versus film, subtlety versus drama, Mozart versus Wagner. Peter Goin's all-encompassing and clear-eyed view captures a hill in the interior Coast Ranges on the horizon and the precision with which the field is organized. The emerald green rows of lettuce seem to reach out to the mountains becoming more delicate and thread-like as they recede into the far distance. The tractor wheels fit perfectly in spaces between the rows and slowly move the machine like a locomotive shunting cars in a railroad yard. Goin gives us a deadpan full-frontal view of this green contraption moving toward us, its two long and fragile arms extend across eight rows on either side and emit a magical mist. The white tanks mounted on both sides of the tractor hold liquid pesticide, but they could also be the two giant eyes of an enormous insect imagined by H.G. Wells. Goin's visual humor transforms his clear-eyed and informative photograph into a terrifying narrative about an alien "spray bug" with an appetite for lettuce that landed in Salinas, "the Salad Bowl of the USA." To make this photograph and the many others in this Keepsake, it seems to me Goin had to crouch down and immerse himself in the agricultural activities he was observing. Unlike Adams, Goin is not searching for a subject that best fits a preconceived vision and style. He is intimately interested in what is in front of him. In doing so, Goin can take the seemingly ordinary and present us with something extraordinary while preserving the documentary aspect of the photograph.

Record of Grace Aaggie Pietertje, # 271

Of the innumerable documents and photographs pertaining to the Bancroft's collections on agriculture, none seems more earnest yet whimsical than this page reproduced from a ledger book belonging to Otis H. Lockhart. It lists in a small, crabbed, but neat hand each of his dairy cows by name—in this case Grace Aaggie Pieteerje—date of birth, average yearly milk production, weight, lineage—extending back at least two generations —and sale. Each page has an accompanying photograph pasted down on the upper left corner that reminds me of Bancroft's "mug shot" books from the prisons at Folsom and San Quentin where a photographic likeness of the prisoner is accompanied by a handwritten description of the type of crime, length of sentence, attributes, and physical measurements. Perhaps the most poignant part of this bovine book is the scrawled declaration in pencil at the top of the page, "Sold to Rhoades."

A Birds-eye View on the Cattle Ranch of Daniel McCarty

In the 1860s, the cattle industry in California suffered devastating losses from drought, overgrazing, and the failure of ranchers to modernize. The surviving cattle farmers instituted a number of improvements such as new breeding and feed techniques that raised the weight of yearlings by as much as two hundred pounds. Gone were the large, unfenced Spanish-style ranchos; instead farmers constructed a series of enclosed spaces in which they could control breeding and grazing. Gone too were the Rowdy Yates (as played by a young Clint Eastwood) drovers from *Rawhide* replaced by the railroad running through the McCarty Ranch. Getting livestock products to the markets required fast and efficient transportation, which was just as important in the 1880s as it is today.

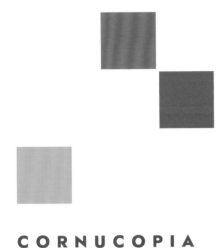

CORNUCOPIA

WITHIN THE HUNDRED MILLION ACRES OF CALIFORNIA is more concentrated and diverse agricultural bounty than any place else in the world—as many as 450 products. Twenty distinct plantings can be seen in a dozen miles of Salinas Valley driving. Turkey coops, emu corrals, dairy yards, fields serving the cut-flower business, and foothill rangeland hold varied livestock. An orchard might contain eight different olives, or a single vineyard block a dozen grape varieties that are not only cherished but fought over by winemakers who want to lock up access to what they might perceive as a crucial component in a Bordeaux- or Rhone-style blend. It was, after all, wines from California that featured in the famed 1976 "Judgment of Paris," which pitted Napa, Sonoma, and Santa Cruz cabernet sauvignon and

chardonnay against the best of Bordeaux and Burgundy—and saw California wines emerge as stars. French wine critics forty years later are still restive and chastened.

In unlikely places in California (but for good reason) are found important crops: nursery stock, flowers, avocados, and heirloom vegetables in rapidly urbanizing North County San Diego. In Monterey County are acre upon acre of lettuce and artichokes, strawberries and arugula, cruciferous vegetables and selective oddities like the nopales (pads) of the prickly pear (*Opuntia*) cactus and their delectable tunas, red fruit, harvested roasted and eaten. Apricots near Patterson are gone, displaced by urbanization advancing at a rate so fast it could be steroid-stimulated. Or there are dates, growing at a leisurely pace in Mecca and the Coachella Valley in southeastern Riverside County. These are not small-value crops. Raised around California in 2015 was better than $2.3 billion of lettuce (three-quarters of the U.S. total); strawberry crops earned more than $2.4 billion (2014). In the San Joaquin Valley's hugely fertile counties are almonds, peaches, plums, apricots, pistachios and pomegranates, melons, oranges, and grapes. A bounty; maybe even a cornucopia.

Yet added people augurs change: a diverse population shapes a varied agriculture. The human population of California has doubled in the last century, redoubled, doubled, doubled, and redoubled yet again. In 1900, the count of California residents topped a million; in 2018, we number 40 million. This produces a familiar story. Cities form and are fed by the countryside, aided by the capital investments of savvy urban entrepreneurs who understand how critical a reliable food supply is—and how great the profits can be from agricultural products, exports, processed foods, and even the winery and restaurant industry. The names of individuals and firms involved are legends and the actions not always angelic, but they are

the backbone of California agriculture and, because of that, intriguing and innovative, challenging and costly. A cornucopia, indeed.

Growth is awry, however, with the Central Coast and interior regions such as the Sacramento-San Joaquin valleys growing more speedily than the big metropolitan regions of the Southland and the chock-full San Francisco Bay Area. This puts special pressure on agricultural producers, a longstanding tendency in California. The author Joan Didion, a Sacramento native and Berkeley graduate (1956), remarked in the 1960s on the disappearance of farmland. She was not alone, then or more recently, in voicing alarm at the displacement of cropland by industry and a world of housing cul-de-sacs. The American Farmland Trust has long fretted about and documented a loss of agricultural land in California, as it's submerged under pavement and suburban lawn. The same is true now near Davis and Fresno, Porterville and Modesto, as it once was with Riverside and Pasadena and Petaluma and Mecca.

The relationship between city and countryside constitutes far more than a favored theme of social theorists. As cities expand—and a human population that grows more than thirty times in something more than a century constitutes expansion and then some—they occupy surrounding territory. This is a movement that John Fraser Hart describes as the "perimetropolitan bow wave," borrowing imagery from a seagoing vessel whose huge displacement shoves aside water from the boat's bow as it motors forward. Agricultural uses are similarly tucked out of the way as cities, suburbs, and exurban ranchettes radiate from a city center. Competition develops for the crucial resources of soil, water, labor, land, and energy—all contributors to the agricultural cornucopia of California.

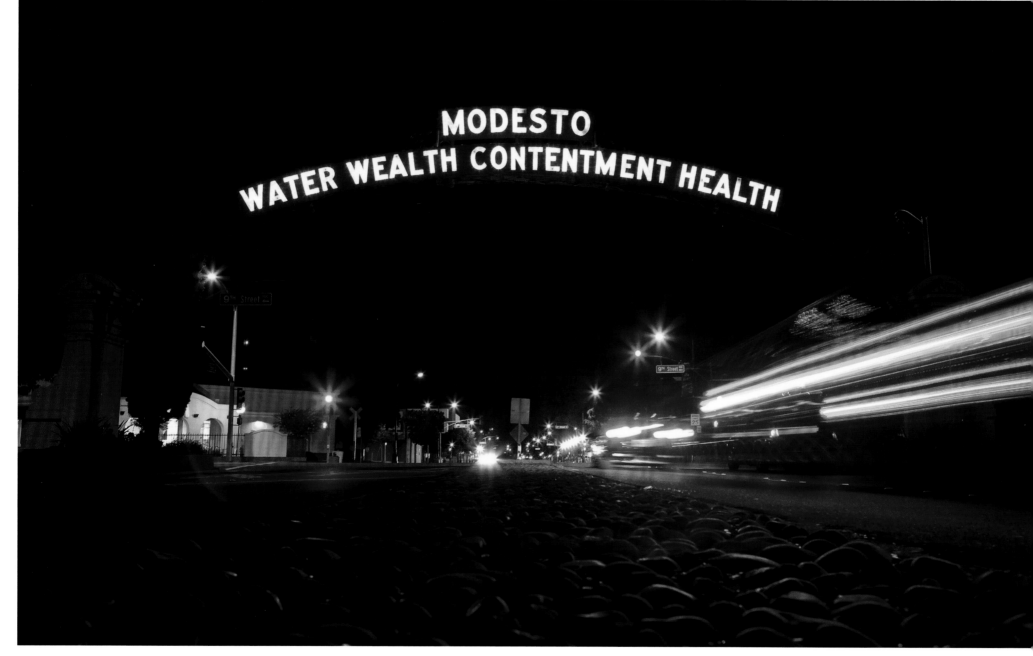

"Water, Wealth, Contentment, Health," Arch, Modesto, 2008, Peter Goin.

BANC DIG 2017.14:Ag01138

Heliotrope Sunflowers: Horizon View of Sunflower field, Colusa County, 2006, Peter Goin.

"Water, Wealth, Contentment, Health," Arch, Modesto

The wording of Modesto's welcoming arch nearly says it all for this community whose substance and wealth through the last 160 years is strongly tied to agriculture, including marketing, finance, processing—and the control of water. Yet Modesto is home to a widely varied community of small farmer-producers, many of them families and recent immigrants who maintain a smaller-scale agricultural production that is marketed at fruit stands, U-pick fields, and rural stands operated on the honor system, where a customer selects fruit or vegetables and leaves payment in a basket or piggy-bank. The city of Modesto, with a sizable population of more than 200,000 residents in the San Joaquin Valley and long an agricultural center, proudly shares its motto and a sense of pride. Modesto is anything but alone. Greeting signs appear at the entrance to many a California town: Castroville, Artichoke Center of the World; Half Moon Bay, Pumpkin Capital; Arvin: Garden in the Sun; Sacramento, California, America's Farm-to-Fork Capital; and even today, although much of the garlic crop grown has migrated east to Fresno and Kern counties, there is Gilroy, Garlic Capital of the World—and home every summer to a multi-day garlic festival. Repeat after us: Anyone need garlic ice cream?

Brown Turkey Fig, Ficus carica, *Monrovia Growers in Woodlake,* 2006, Peter Goin.

Heliotrope Sunflowers: Horizon View of Sunflower field, Colusa County

With its sun-following head a sight familiar to backyard gardeners, a vast field of sunflowers in full oil-seed production mode is startling. We may react one way to a few sunflowers, but with altogether another response when greeted by 100,000 of them, acre-upon-acre. California's agricultural landscapes abound in ever-dramatic vistas, stretching seemingly to the horizon. Consider an endless view of the great puff-ball flowers marking a field of mature onions; walnut trees with a canopy so dense sunlight barely enters; or an alfalfa field grown tall with purple flowers and the heady scent of wet earth, flowing water, and hay awaiting harvest. These are sights to keep travelers awake and looking for more.

Brown Turkey Fig

Hailing from Asia, but cultivated since ancient times in the Middle East, figs do well in a Mediterranean climate, and in addition to commercial production, are a popular garden tree, bearing once or twice a year. Tolerant of various growing conditions, the trees have naturalized to California environments, which means they can survive and be spread around the state's temperate climes with relatively little care. Dwarf figs are often kept as ornamental trees, but some fig variants can grow skyward to 30 feet height or more. While it can be argued that nursery and greenhouse-grown crops are not necessarily "agricultural," the United States Department of Agriculture and California County Agricultural Commissioners, required to file annual crop reports, each beg to differ, since "nursery and greenhouse crops" are actually the third largest agricultural income producer, after "milk and cream" and grapes.

Vaunted Harvest—The Cornucopia

Dominated visually by the Buddha's hand fingered citron, a dramatic and distinctive presence often used to perfume a room—or vodka—this was a scene in 2006 greeting visitors to the annual open house at the University of California's Lindcove Research and Extension Center. The fruits showcased are varied—citron, pomelo, mandarins (formerly "tangerines"), Cuties, Satsumas, grapefruit, lemons, limes, loquats and kumquats, and of course, blood, navel and Valencia oranges.

Juniperus Mint Julep®

No small part of agricultural innovation in California comes from crops deemed successful in other venues that are sought after and tested in a California setting. Unsurprisingly, agricultural nurseries are often ahead of the game in terms of finding ornamentals or fruiting-crops that can make the transition to California's largely Mediterranean-type climate—summer-dry and winter-wet (hopefully). This peculiar array is an exotic set of junipers.

California Prune Orchard in Blossom Time, Sorosis Farm

There is ample reason for the Japanese (and American) enthusiasm for fruit trees fully in blossom. While it is cherry trees (and often ornamental varieties) that bring delegations of mouth-agape tourists to urban destinations, in the groves throughout California, almond trees flower first, and prune trees follow with swift and copious blossoms. Prunes were long a steady California feature, although the crop's currently preferred term is "French plum" rather than prune, reflecting a bit of industry difficulty in marketing to a younger age cohort. The significance of orchard crops (prunes included) is long recognized in California. Irrigation water shortages in the San Joaquin Valley have stressed growers of almonds, pomegranates, and pistachios. Those trees do require regular watering, while amid a drought and restricted water deliveries, fields can simply be left unplanted. And these trees flourished at the urban fringe: arriving in California from Sicily at the end of the 19th century, the Teresi family acquired a small but successful holding. Curiously, this early print includes a reference to the Peninsula Interurban Railroad, which threaded through the Santa Clara Valley near the Sorosis Farm (and later, Sorosis Fruit Company).

California Prune Orchard in Blossom Time, Sorosis Farm, Seen from the Interurban R.R., Alice Iola Hare.

Albumen print. Alice Iola Hare Photograph Collection.

Vaunted Harvest—The Cornucopia, Arranged at the Lindcove Research Orchard, 2006, Peter Goin.

Juniperus *Mint Julep® at Monrovia Growers, Woodlake,* 2006, Peter Goin.

Almond Grove, 2008, Peter Goin.

Almond Grove

This almond grove lies within San Joaquin County, but almonds are found all through the Sacramento and San Joaquin valleys. California produces 82 percent of the almonds consumed worldwide, harvesting approximately 800,000 acres across a 400-mile stretch from northern Tehama County to southern Kern County (2014). Approximately nine percent of California's agricultural water is dedicated to almond farming, about the same as many other tree crops, but with such a sizable acreage, still a respectable consumer of irrigation water. There are nearly 6,800 almond farms in California, and 91 percent of these are family farms. From a visual point of view, almond groves provide a unique opportunity to witness multiple vantage points within a single view, a metaphoric testimonial to the complexity of California's agriculture ventures.

Pumpkins, 1890–1893

The pumpkin, among the relatively few agricultural crops native to North America, is understandably a crowd favorite, and tellingly pumpkins are among a handful of agricultural crops that households regularly purchase, bring home, decorate, and put on exhibit. The tradition goes way back, putatively to the origins of Thanksgiving, that most American of holiday celebrations. Pumpkins do well as field crops around California, with these robust specimens in the vicinity of Santa Maria and Santa Barbara earning attention from an admirer.

Pumpkins, 1890–1893, Norman H. Reed, N.H. Reed Photograph Album of Santa Barbara and Vicinity.

BANC PIC 2012.089—fALB

"How Much Do You Think This Pumpkin Weighs?"

While Santa Clara and San Mateo counties were once agricultural strongholds in the San Francisco Bay Area, much of that agriculture is gone, now, replaced by the knowledge economy and innovation engines of Silicon Valley. There are, however, some holdouts, including the Uesugi Farms, with fields and an annual pumpkin lot. The variety of pumpkins—from the huge specimens used in competition to the super-sugar snack varieties prized by bakers of homemade pumpkin pies—make such spots a fall destination, as families travel to pick out a favored pumpkin or two for carving and jack-o-lanterns. For nearly 30 years, the Pumpkin Park has featured the Pumpkinville Railroad.

"How Much Do You Think This Pumpkin Weighs?" Uesugi Farms. The Storybook Path, Pumpkin Pete's Enchanted Hayride and a Cow Train, 2006, Peter Goin.

An "East Side" Sierra grazing scene, Paul Fair (?), M.W. Talbot Collection of Forestry and Agriculture Photographs.

BANC PIC 1979.084—085B

An "East Side" Sierra grazing scene

Sheep, goats, cattle, horses: in California today remain active users of nearly half the area of the state that is classified as "rangeland"—meaning areas that for whatever reason (topography, sparse water, elevation, limited access) are not considered suitable as timber-growing sites, or as venues for tree- or field-crops. In the eastern Sierra, starting in the 1850s, long grazing movements of sheep from the summer-dry lands of Southern California brought huge bands of sheep, numbering sometimes in the thousands of animals, up the east side of the Sierra Nevada where they would eventually cross over a Sierra pass and then return along the western foothills of the Sierra to Bakersfield or other sheep-friendly destinations. Rants from observers like John Muir (though himself paradoxically once a sheepherder) decried "hooved locusts." But not until designation in the 1890s of uplands in the Sierra into what would prove to be nine National Forests did trailing movements along stock driveways truly slow.

Goats in pasture, McCormack Ranch, Montezuma Hills, Solano County

Often curious, but skittish too, gregarious goats like to travel in a bunch, and are sometimes skeptical of interlopers. On grain farms and pastures around California, goats, sheep, and cattle earn their keep in part by consuming agricultural aftermath: seeds, stalks, and grain that might fall to the ground during harvest. Bit by bit, communities are starting to bring in herds for short-term but intense vegetation management: goats eat shrubs that otherwise can pose a sizable risk of carrying wildfires through woodlands or housing tracts. These Boer goats, a hefty but charismatic meat breed, are of a mind to seek out other fare, or at least escape from their admirers, in this hill view just north of the Sacramento River near Rio Vista.

Goats in pasture, McCormack Ranch, Montezuma Hills, Solano County, 2007, Peter Goin.

Turkeys, San Joaquin County, California, ca. 1910. Gelatin silver print. From the album "Views of El Solyo Ranch, Vernalis, California."

Close view, Poultry sheds, East Avenue, East of Turlock, Merced County, 2006, Peter Goin.

THE VINTAGE IN CALIFORNIA—AT WORK AT THE WINE-PRESSES.—Drawn by P. Frenzeny.—[See Page 790]

The Vintage in California, at Work at the Wine Presses. Engraving on paper. Robert B. Honeyman, Jr. Collection of Early Californian and Western American Pictorial Material, Paul Frenzeny (1840–1902).

Close-up of red wine grapes, Armida Winery, west of Healdsburg, Sonoma County, California, 2007, Peter Goin.

BANC DIG 2017.14:Ag00268

View of top-loading bin, dropping Pinot Noir grapes into crush machinery, Armida Winery, 2007, Peter Goin.

BANC DIG 2017.14:Ag00998

Hand of Self-designated "wine mistress" directing flow tube of Pinot Noir grapes after crush, Armida Winery, 2007, Peter Goin.

BANC DIG 2017.14:Ag00999c

Pomace, or Marc Grape Skins and Stems Removed in the De-stemming and Crushing Process, Awaiting Disposal, 2007, Peter Goin.

BANC DIG 2017.14:Ag001001a

Turkeys, San Joaquin County, California, ca. 1910
In the here and now, California turkey growers and the poultry industry at large tend to be skeptical of public visits and oversight. But turkeys, especially 100 years ago, were relatively robust creatures, and even amenable to herding—seen here on a San Joaquin County turkey ranch, with a horseback-mounted rider at the rear and ranch hands at the side to prevent runaways. Such "turkey drives" were by no means uncommon, as were trailing drives to a sales yard or market of—you name it—pigs, sheep, goats, and (of course) cattle.

Close view, Poultry sheds
While a studious look from a light plane or Google Earth of the foothills of Stanislaus or San Joaquin counties has long spotted long linear sheds where poultry is raised, on the ground increasingly those sites are surrounded by chain-link fences with stern signage, including "No Trespassing" placards threatening exposure to biohazards. Consumers show an increasing willingness to pay more per dozen for eggs or meat where packaging promises "free range" or "cage free" existence for the flocks within. The humane agriculture movement is especially attuned to ducks and turkeys and chickens—whether layers, roasters, or broilers—and argues for room to move and, in some cases, raising heritage breeds that can bring a premium price.

The Vintage in California, at Work at the Wine Presses
A harvest free-for-all is evident in this action-filled image, part of the massive Honeyman Collection at The Bancroft Library. In the details lie considerable charm: top right, workers with hair queues (bianzi 辮子) and broad hats in the characteristic style of Chinese laborers stomp boxes of grapes to send precious juice into large barrels for fermentation; others labor at the wine press, while baskets of grapes await unloading in a wagon at front-left. The wine press gears are being turned with human power, even as mules alongside a huge barn patiently wait for the grape-laden baskets to be unloaded. It's a scene of industry and potential profit captured in one frenetic vista.

Close-up of red wine grapes; View of top-loading bin; Hand of self-designated "wine mistress"; Pomace, or Marc Grape Skins and Stems
No time is more demanding at a winery than the crush. An era of hand-destemming incoming grape clusters and foot-stomping them in vats to release juice has largely ended, replaced by pricey shiny machines that speed the process with only a fraction of the previous investment required in labor. Picked into 35-pound lugs and then consolidated into half-ton bins for transport to a winery, grapes are crushed, with the resulting liquid must pumped into containers for early fermentation. So is commenced the wine-making process, worth billions of dollars to the California economy. It will take a year or up to three for bottled wine to make it into a winery tasting room or the cavernous showrooms of major wine emporia.

Among the pioneers of research into California landscape change and agriculture was UC Berkeley geographer James J. Parsons (1915–1997), who officially taught in the department from 1948–1986, but in fact continued graduating PhD students well into the 1990s. A first published paper in 1940 was on the growing of hops in California (think: Hopland, California, and today's Hop Kiln Winery), but his orbit of interest would expand throughout the state, culminating in a photographic essay (with Paul F. Starrs) on agriculture in the San Joaquin Valley, and, not long after, this work on the stunningly diverse landscapes and people who inhabit them in the interior of the state.

James J. Parsons, "A Geographer Looks at the San Joaquin Valley" Reprint and text from *Geographical Review*, October, 1986, GF504.C2P3 1986: For me few places are more exciting than California's San Joaquin Valley, especially on a blistering hot afternoon in late summer. It has been called 'the world's richest agricultural valley,' a technological miracle of productivity where dog-eat-dog competition is at its finest. My focus is the southern part of the Central Valley of California, that alluvium-filled structural trough between the Coast Ranges and the Sierra that stretches for more than 400 miles from Redding to the Tehachapis. The northern third of the Central Valley, drained by the Sacramento River, is smaller and better watered, more Anglo-Saxon, and much less populous than the San Joaquin portion. It lacks the landscape of cotton fields, vineyards, orange groves, and oil fields that are so symbolic of the latter.

Cannabis Grow Site in the Emerald Triangle

The total crop value is, to put it lightly, "contested." Prices to growers and users are all over the map, as California and other states attempt to find a production and taxation middle ground that will prove acceptable to all concerned. While no County Agricultural Commissioner's Report includes a reliable account of how much the California cannabis crop is worth, estimates for 2018 run between $10 and $25 billion, totaling both black market and legal sales. Different purchasers (or backyard growers) seek different results, from pain relief to better sleep to a benevolent high, and the technology and cultivation techniques involved are formidable. Cannabis is being squeezed through a slowly implemented tracking system, at least for the relatively small percentage of registered legal growers, with taxation at every turn. The legal scene affecting cannabis growing includes city regulations, county rules, state-level legislation, and then the changeable and sometimes inscrutable actions of the federal government. In 2018—and time brings change— cannabis production is a negotiation between a high-tech agricultural crop and a drug grown and sold in the face of enduring suspicion and resistance. Sites will divert water illegally, lay out poisons to get rid of rodents that can kill the raptors and scavengers who eat them, open space on hilltops as grow sites are prepared, and can pose a hazard to public lands hikers and other travelers. And cannabis is, without much credible argument in opposition, almost certainly the single largest-value crop in California agriculture—now legal for both medical and recreational use.

Cannabis Grow Site with Distant Horizon, in the Emerald Triangle, 2007, Peter Goin.

BANC DIG 2017.14:Ag00962

AT WORK IN THE FIELDS

WE ALL EAT. WHO WORKS CALIFORNIA'S FIELDS AND RANGELANDS? Who is caretaker, cultivator, steward, tender, harvester of the foods we eat? A 1980s cartoon showed a happy Los Angeles resident, with just the right text: Southern California, Watch it grow 50 times!—Just add water. More sustenance than that is needed. Finding a supply of workers to work on croplands and ranches is a source of concern; many laborers who used to be paid by the day are now hired for months at a time, or year-round. A 2016 study by UC Davis agricultural economist Philip Martin and colleagues, working Social Security records, counted some 829,000 California farmworkers. While recent changes in California and federal law require proof of identification and penalize employers who hire undocumented workers, with an upswing in the number and intensity of federal immigration audits, it is no easy matter making a precise count of men and women at work in matters agricultural. Since statehood, farmworkers routinely come from abroad, with Hispanic ranch hands and field cultivators, irrigators, and harvesters ever since 1769 when Mission San Diego de Alcalá was established in San Diego. Sure, we all eat. Who, though protects, picks, packs, and prepares what becomes our meals?

The skills and requirements of a labor pool take many forms across a 250-year history. Native Americans, brought into the Mission system in circumstances barely removed from slavery, were a crucial part of feeding communities gathered into the orbit of the California missions to meet economic and Church religious goals. Other groups went to work: discharged soldiers; arriving visitors from Europe or the East Coast of the U.S.; a steady yield of incoming migrants from the great length of Latin America; arrivals from Asia who came to California in the 1800s and 1900s as contract workers or on their own, seeking jobs and potential prosperity. But with the Overland Route of the transcontinental Union Pacific Railroad completed in 1869, legislation quickly passed in the California Legislature to bar furloughed Chinese railroad workers from mining, so they turned to other toil, building levees in the Sacramento-San Joaquin Delta, or assembling long rock walls, still evident on ranchlands in the Sierra Nevada foothills. Sometimes entrepreneurial farm ownership beckoned. More often, work laboring on farms was available, but little more. The raw conditions were hardly beneficent; wages paid tended to match the austere circumstances provided in terms of housing, transportation, diet, and healthcare. Little wonder that farm workers and labor organizers tried to improve conditions, but violence during protests and formal strikes pitted growers against their own workers, sometimes replacing entire groups with newcomers who growers believed might be less inclined to resist. When ag workers began to gain earnings enough to acquire land of their own, California growers and lawmakers sought federal government intervention with legislation to make land ownership difficult or actively illegal, and the Chinese Exclusion Act (1882) and the Geary Act (1892) sought to block Chinese immigration, the first of a long series of exclusionary laws directed against a specific racial or ethnic group.

Life near active farming brings bothers: land-tilling, seeding and spraying, water shepherded and steered. But few subjects are more contentious, more life-affecting, or so economically costly as the availability and conditions of farm labor in California. Much of that labor pool historically came from Mexico or other locations south of the border, and in researching the *Field Guide to California Agriculture*, all but a couple of our field-side discussions were conducted in Spanish. Programs to bring in laborers are well intentioned, through California history, and in the current economy, seasonal field workers are especially hard to come by since many returned to their homelands. The housing provided for agricultural workers is at times of high quality with amenities. At other sites, such is not the case, which unsurprisingly makes it more difficult to find, and keep, good workers. As xenophobia and the overall labor supply ebbs and flows, Hispanic workers (variously Latino, Chicano/a, Hispano, Mexican) come to California, or leave to return home; crossing borders is common. Legislation seeks to improve living and working conditions, though sometimes benefiting the agricultural producers more than the laborers. The story is a long one, and the histories of labor and the agricultural economy in California draw on Bancroft Library materials and tell a tale with plenty of ups and downs.

Meal Break, Farm Workers, Bean Fields in Monterey County, 2006, Peter Goin.

Meal Break, Farm Workers, Bean Fields in Monterey County

Considering how crucial workers are in the world of cultivation and harvest in California, it may surprise no one that many of the issues that agriculture brings to the fore concern acceptable working conditions: Is potable water readily available? Are there field-side portable toilets and sanitary facilities? Is housing suitable, and safe transport readily at hand? Will children find schooling easily? Are employers and labor contractors aboveboard? Still, there is often time for community and camaraderie. Here, workers enjoy a lunch break at a bean field in Monterey County.

Night Meeting at the Crossroads, Cotton Strike, Great Central Valley, California

With darkness well upon them, strikers meet to organize a plan of action. Sporadic labor actions, often led by the relatively militant Cannery and Agricultural Workers Industrial Union, began in 1930, but gained effectiveness through the decade. Actual strikes generally came as harvest season arrived, beginning in August, and the most formidable of the 1933 strikes was in cotton fields of the San Joaquin Valley, where somewhere between 12,000 and 18,000 harvest workers were employed. Identified strikers were often ousted from company-owned housing, and sometimes management officials were deputized. In October 1933, two strikers were killed in the town of Pixley, another died in nearby Arvin, and eight more were wounded. In just 1933 some thirty labor actions involved nearly 50,000 agricultural workers, and some strike organizers were charged under the red-baiting California Criminal Syndicalism Act of 1919—which went un-repealed until 1991. *Bitter Harvest*—the title of Cletus Daniel's study of California farmworkers, drew on Bancroft Library materials and was published in 1982 by UC Press, setting a solid standard for examining the difficulties of seasonal labor.

Kern County, ca. 1887

If working conditions for agricultural workers in the late nineteenth century would be considered austere by our standards now, housing could be no less a problem. In an 1887 view, the photographer Carleton Watkins visited Kern County, which along with Kings and Kaweah counties were at the foot of the San Joaquin Valley. The lodging was a handful of cots, set out underneath a small grove of eucalyptus trees. The farm where they were working showcased an obvious prosperity—look at the barn. Sleeping out of doors in heat that frequently reaches 100°F. in summer, with cold and rain in a good winter, would be a challenge.

Kern County, ca. 1887, Carleton Watkins. Albumen print. Keith-McHenry-Pond family pictorial collection.

BANC PIC 1952.002:4

Hired Man and Hoverly Children, Imperial Valley
While conditions across the U.S. in the 1930s were difficult and sometimes desperate, there were earlier images of rural need and poverty. In California, perhaps unsurprisingly, among the chief victims of agricultural poverty were children. In this image acquired by an unknown photographer about 1900, the children's stance and dress bespeak a difficult life.

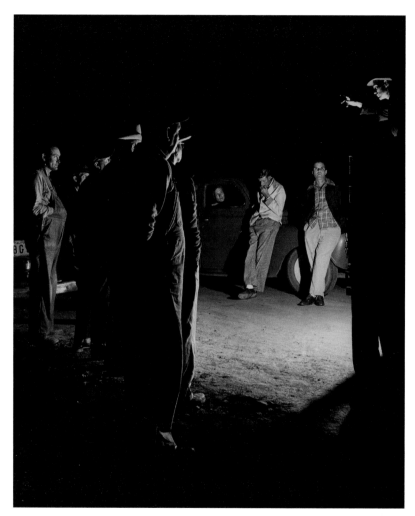

Night Meeting at the Crossroads, Cotton Strike, Great Central Valley, California, 1933, Hansel Mieth. Gelatin silver print. Printed in 1998 for the Mother Jones International Fund for Documentary Photography.

BANC PIC 2003.040—AX

Hired Man and Hoverly Children, Imperial Valley, ca. 1903, Unknown photographer, Gelatin silver print.

BANC PIC 19xx.054:10—PIC

***Mexican Migratory Farm Worker Housing... Migrant agricultural
worker's family... Migrant's Home... Home of Oklahoma Drought***
With the Great Depression, the Dust Bowl, and the so-called
Okie migration all hitting in the 1930s, a lot was wrong with
agriculture and the larger world of environmental change in
the United States. If it was possible to get to California, with
its burgeoning need for field workers and harvesters, a new
work force just might be put to work. Rarely, though, were
living and working conditions uplifting, as photographs of
these shanties suggest. Improvisation might, for some, turn
camping into housing, but conditions were rugged or worse.
Federal workers traveled California, documenting migrant
harvesters, hoboes, tramps, and bindlestiffs, creating a
daunting record echoed by writers of the Works Progress
Administration (WPA). Certainly *The Grapes of Wrath* (1939,
Pulitzer Prize) by John Steinbeck (Nobel Prize, Literature,
1962) and a subsequent 1940 film, directed by John Ford
(Best Director Academy Award), shot the plight of refugee
emigrants into a sharp focus. Photographers working for the
Resettlement Administration and Farm Security Administration
(FSA) captured a hardscrabble existence. Few photographs
are so memorable as the sequence taken by Dorothea Lange
with a Graflex camera and 4x5 inch film. Her 1936 images of
Florence Owens Thompson and children at an encampment
of pea-harvesters in Nipomo, north of Los Angeles, are
deservedly considered definitive images documenting
the Great Depression and its effects. After photographing
the "migrant mother" and children in their lean-to, Lange
continued north and publicized the plight of the camp-
dwellers, which led relief authorities to deliver some 20,000
pounds of food to agricultural camp residents, many of whom
were eating vegetables gleaned from frozen fields after an
uncharacteristic cold snap that also eclipsed local harvest
work. The FSA archives remain among the great public
histories in American life (available free online from the
Library of Congress).

Mexican Migratory Farm Worker Housing. Dorothea Lange.
Gelatin Silver Print. Farm Security Administration Photograph Collection.
BANC PIC 1942.008 Folder 102, Part 2 #16439E

Migrant agricultural worker's family. Seven hungry children. Father a native Californian, 1936.
Dorothea Lange. Gelatin silver print. National Council on Agricultural Life and Labor photographs.
BANC PIC 1967.047

Worker housing, mid-town Firebaugh, 2006, Peter Goin.

Planada Village Directory Sign [worker housing], 2008, Peter Goin.

Migrant's Home, February 1937. Gelatin silver print. Transferred from the Ralph W. Hollenberg materials relating to the Farm Security Administration, Regional Office IX, San Francisco records.

BANC PIC 1942.008:37:3 box 3

Home of Oklahoma Drought Refugees, February 1936, Dorothea Lange. Gelatin silver print. Farm Security Photograph Collection.

BANC PIC 1942.008; Folder 102, Part 2 #1811

Worker housing, mid-town Firebaugh... Planada Village Directory Sign [worker housing]

Spotting farmworker housing is not always predictable or obvious. But identifying agricultural worker housing in the here and now is easy enough: it's distinctive. With perhaps a million agricultural workers in California, finding suitable and safe living spaces is rarely easy. Some worker housing is provided by growers themselves, bumped by state law, encouraged by farm labor activists, and simply recognizing that a permanent workforce deserves acceptable living conditions. Some of the housing is better-quality than others, and when the quality is good, the pickers and their accompanying children may find a clean ordered place with stores and schools nearby. Not always. Much of California's farm labor needs are seasonal, which speaks to a migration up and down the West Coast, from Yakima's hopfields and orchards of apple, pear, and cherry trees to the vineyards of the Willamette Valley to the supply of workers needed for cultivation and harvest of the hundreds of crops raised and shipped from California.

July 1936. Kern County, Kern Lake District, Frick Ranch. Laborer's Cabins. Photographer unknown. Gelatin silver print. The Harry Everett Drobish papers.

Red Worker Houses, Uses Found beyond Living Quarters, 2007, Peter Goin.

July 1936. Kern County, Kern Lake District, Frick Ranch.
Laborer's Cabins

A set of southern San Joaquin Valley "laborer's cabins" could provide shelter and an element of stability; certainly the stout cabins were better than much of what itinerant laborers could find available to them in 1930s California.

Red Worker Houses, Uses Found beyond Living Quarters

A steer, minimally fenced in alongside haphazard housing, is a reminder that farm workers have their own needs, problems, and communities. Dirt roads, generations of housing, decayed to a suspect standard, and a constant need to keep moving mean workers rarely can call anyplace a stable "home," although conditions in the last twenty or so years have improved somewhat. Living in doubt about legal status, an uncertainty about children and their education, and a makeshift existence add up to an encumbered and hand-to-mouth existence.

Single Worker House, Abandoned, Cattlemen Road

Set on a flattened triangle of land alongside Cattlemen Road in Monterey County is worker housing that reflects good original intentions but an uncertain execution and maintenance. The pre-World War Two buildings, vaguely Art Deco-styled, are constructed to a reasonable quality if poorly maintained, and house an active colony of immigrant agricultural workers in the southern Salinas Valley. Some residents have strung together woven-wire pens that corral a steer or two, and the community as a whole sustains a flock of poultry that scratches a makeshift living from weeds and seeds and insects among the buildings. Surrounded by lettuce and broccoli fields, there is crop wealth all around, but that does not necessarily filter down to residents in the worker camps. Newer housing for farm workers tends to be built to a higher quality, but is not always available, especially in areas where there is a long history of ranch- and crop-agriculture with housing stock that is aging and in slow decay.

Single Worker House, Abandoned, Cattlemen Road, Monterey County, 2007, Peter Goin.

BANC DIG 2017.14:Ag00759

DIVERSITY

VARIATION, INVENTIVE AND FAR-REACH-ING, IS THE BYWORD OF CALIFORNIA AGRICULTURE. That diversity owes much to climate. California is one of the six regions in the world with a reliably Medi-terranean-type climate: bone dry in summers; **hopefully wet in winter and spring.** Some crops grow well where it's summer-dry. Others require irrigation and in California, agriculture—and city-dwellers—need water in summer. That means two things: first, irrigation is needed; second, California is a world apart from farming tradition or practice east of the Rockies. And the diversity of agriculture owes much to a husbanding of field crops, orchards, groves, and livestock that originated as mainstays feeding cities near the Mediterranean Sea, from Seville to Damascus. Much was learned, borrowed, and tried with success. Other crops were flops. Agricultural diversity has world-wide debts, especially to other regions where novel crops can be found, such as Latin America, from whom we get avocado, maize, tomatoes, chili peppers, and spices. Modern eating is all about the Columbian Exchange, shaping a culinary tradeoff of Old World and New World.

The first change came early. Livestock ranching in Alta California during the Spanish-Mexican era, for example, was in an utterly characteristic "buckaroo" style—the word an Americanization of the Spanish "vaquero"—rather than embracing the austere dress, demeanor, and working gear of the cowboy from Texas or the Plains. Subsidized U.S. crops like soybeans, corn, and other grains that east of the Rockies receive billions of dollars of federal Farm Bill subsidies are a limited contributor to California's agricultural production (under ten percent, in value). Instead, what used to be called "minor crops" and are now referred to as "specialty crops." While fruit from La Conchita's Seaside Banana Garden after a series of landslides is no longer extant, there is talk in Goleta (a Santa Barbara neighbor) of a homegrown and pricey brand-new California coffee crop. Cannabis production alone, now legal for in-state medicinal and recreational consumption, is valued at $14—35 billion, although precise figures are impossible to find since the value and size of the cannabis crop involves guesswork.

The tally of crops where California grows 99% of United States production is impressive: almonds, artichokes, dates, figs, raisin grapes, kiwifruit, olives, clingstone peaches, pistachios, dried plums, pomegranates, and walnuts. Even "traditional" California crops (asparagus), are relatively rare crops in the view of the USDA and agribusiness producers in other states. Atop the ledger, entries tallying agricultural income are milk and dairy, almonds, cattle and calves, nursery and greenhouse crops, grapes, strawberries, oranges and other citrus (lemons are a top-15 crop in farm-gate value), and even asparagus, broccoli, spinach, and leafy vegetables are worth tens of millions of dollars. Official estimates show a farm-gate production of $47 billion in 2015. Recent and more experimental crops coming onto the commercial agriculture scene are speculative, as they always have been, but with a vast proportion of California's agricultural production exported to other states or abroad (26% in 2015), much of the diversity of the United States diet is attributable to one place: California.

Important alternative agricultural products tend to be those raised using techniques that depart from the conventional—in scale, style, technique, or market. Organic producers have always been a part of California agriculture, but rarely were they sizable contributors, in dollar value, to the agricultural receipts tallied yearly by county agricultural commissioners. That changed as both producers and consumers in the 1970s recognized the role of food in healthier living and embraced a dramatic back-to-the-land movement. California's rising countercultural interest in soil-building and cultivation techniques like biodynamic agriculture or French-intensive farming techniques gained advocates, conversational volume, economic power—and practitioners who made it happen. Community gardens, farmers markets, community supporter agriculture (CSAs), U-pick operations, farm-side produce stands each satisfied an interest in what is now called farm-to-table dining, where consumers bring meat, vegetables, fruits, or grains home and are reasonably certain that they know where what they are going to eat comes from.

Pistachio growers have done this with success in mass plantings in the San Joaquin Valley, and specialty crops such as Asian greens are raised around California in greenhouses that maintain the semi-tropical and cold-protected temperatures that the plants prefer. Diversity in California agriculture is a matter of size, a matter of investment, a matter of new-found and adapted knowledge, which ties science to scale. ■

The Irrigated Grid of a New Peach Orchard with Sutter Buttes in the Background, 2006. Peter Goin.

BANC DIG 2017.14:Ag00124

The Irrigated Grid of a New Peach Orchard with Sutter Buttes in the Background

If land and water are essentials of agriculture, their meeting place where water works its way across a field is an unvarnished joy, part of an ageless and productive dance. In this view with the Sutter Buttes standing off in the distance—remnants of volcanic necks in the upper Sacramento Valley—the flood-irrigated peach orchard shows a time-tested and internationally familiar geometry of check dams, fruit trees, and thirsty soils that reiterate the need for a carefully diverted and marshaled water supply. "It's all about the control of water," say dissenters with no small accuracy; supporters reply that a fruitful relationship is born in water—and both cadres are accurate in their description of California agriculture. Irrigation systems are remarkably varied and the technology they employ can range from the simple to the hugely complex and costly. Even a flood-irrigated field with check-dams and valves, as here, however, has to be leveled and managed carefully or water is wasted.

Tulare Lake ca. 1938

Early maps of California, like George Goddard's exquisite effort dating from 1857 (itself once reproduced as a Bancroft Keepsake), show a revealing scene in the southern San Joaquin Valley. Rivers now directed toward Sierra Nevada foothill reservoirs in those days freely flowed into what was sometimes labeled the Tulare Valley. They fed a far larger Tulare Lake (at 760 square miles, more than three times the surface area of Lake Tahoe), which brimmed with water into the 1890s. Technically the area is an endorheic basin, which in its day would collect water from the Kern, Tule, Kaweah, and Kings rivers until those overflowed into Tulare Lake. For a time, the Tulare Basin supplied important food for the miners and merchants pouring into Gold Rush era California, with millions of fresh-water turtles gathered, shipped north, and fed to diners at upscale restaurants in Sacramento, Stockton, and the San Francisco Bay Area—a legacy recorded in The Bancroft Library's collection of nineteenth century restaurant menus. By the 1930s much change was afoot: entrepreneurs, including "King of California" J.G. Boswell, based in Corcoran, took up farming on an epic scale. The diversion of feeder-rivers to dams and canals put an end to once-flourishing populations of salmon, otters, turtles, and the "tules" or rushes that provided Tulare Lake its name. In the case of J.G. Boswell, once the largest private owner of farmland in California, the go-to crop was cotton, and for decades the area that was once Tulare Lake was drained, disked, and seeded. Cropping still goes on there, but not a lot else happens now, and certainly the ingredients for turtle soup are few and far between.

Tulare Lake ca. 1938. Gelatin silver print. Agriculture and Flood-Related Photographs from the Miller & Lux Collection.

BANC PIC 1973.056

Trimmed and Topped Trees, West of Vernalis Road, Off Hwy 33, San Joaquin County, 2007, Peter Goin.

Trimmed and Topped Trees, West of Vernalis Road, Off Hwy 33, San Joaquin County

The term "infrastructure" is unwieldy, but accurate. Agriculture in California takes place in a witches' brew of creative land use very much tied to irrigation waters, section roads, and crucial rail connections. A quick excursion from the ever-remarkable California Highway 33 puts a traveler alongside actively farmed fields that today include great groves of citrus, nut trees, and field crop production. The Southern Pacific Railroad, including various sidings, transported a goodly amount of the produce, and its right of way is still prominent on the land. Off to one side in this view are orange trees, their tops and branches carefully trimmed to a uniform height by giant horizontal buzz-saws, the better to allow in sunlight and give harvesters access to the citrus crop.

California Country Life

The Bee newspaper chain was once all but synonymous with the agricultural and political world of the so-called "Great Central Valley" (really, two valleys, drained to the Delta by the Sacramento and San Joaquin rivers). During the throes of the Great Depression, a 1933 Sunday supplement of the *Fresno Bee-Republican* with a masthead advertising "California Country Life" offered plenty of boosterism: "Where the World's Economic Woes Mean Nothing." As immigrants and small farmers struggled, that sentiment might be more than a bit optimistic. But it was given voice.

Map of Miller & Lux, Inc. San Joaquin Valley Lands in Stanislaus, Merced, Madera and Fresno Counties

This remarkable map shows a segment of the San Joaquin Valley portion of a vast ranch and farming empire that was the Miller & Lux Corporation, once totaling 1.5 million acres. Accumulating land and water began in the late nineteenth century and persisted into the 1920s (though Miller died in 1916). Visible here is mostly cropland acreage that ran from Crows Landing, in the Sacramento—San Joaquin Delta region, south to Mendota, Merced, and beyond. This was just a part of the Miller & Lux operations, centered on Los Banos. In a dissertation mining the deep archival resources of the Miller & Lux collection in The Bancroft Library, the historian David Igler writes eloquently about the cattle ranching operations, which ran far north and into neighboring Nevada. Map place names offer a striking testament to hope and expectations: Tranquility, Merced, Modesto, Califa, Riverview. Irrigation colonies were deeply inset into the San Joaquin region, but found corporate competition, with the Miller & Lux headquarters in Dos Palos shown at map center. Surrounding those lands are images of products and activities in a San Joaquin Valley bent on agricultural development.

California Country Life [Sunday Supplement to the *Fresno Bee*]
Fresno, California, July 9, 1933.

Map of Miller & Lux, Inc. San Joaquin Valley Lands in Stanislaus, Merced, Madera and Fresno Counties, ca. 1930.

BANC MSS 70/110 c oversize folders 9C

Pauma Valley View from Sam's Mountain, North County San Diego, Peter Goin.

Recognizing the links of water to land and farming, J. Leroy Nickel, an extraordinary attorney and grey eminence of the Miller & Lux empire, acquired water rights and established irrigation and canal systems through the San Joaquin Valley, making the company's Los Banos headquarters base a place of power. Water rights, in particular, required legal action. After lengthy litigation Miller & Lux corporate disputes over ownership and water use concluded in *Lux v. Haggin*, 69 Cal. 255; 10 P. 674; (1886), which literally redefined California water law. Henry Miller (originally a San Francisco butcher) and Nickel were relentless micromanagers, overseeing nearly everything in starchy letters instructing adjutants across the state.

A 1912 letter by Nickel is illustrative. [J.] Leroy Nickel, Letter to F.W. Holbert [Buttonwillow, California], March 7, 1912, Manuscript, Miller & Lux records, BANC MSS C-G 163, Carton 618:1: "I supposed I had made sufficiently clear to you during my conversation with you that the only instructions at the present time that I deem necessary are that you acquaint yourself fully as to the condition of our livestock which includes cattle, sheep, hogs, and horses, the feed situation, and the manner in which the stock is handled. ... There is really no limit or modification as to the nature of the responsibility we expect you to assume in regard to all of our livestock, and therefore I do not expect you to wait for any orders from me, but to go right ahead, doing the best you are able to do as prompted by your own judgement and foresight."

Pauma Valley View from Sam's Mountain

A view from atop Sam's Mountain shows the spread of Pauma Valley, with field crops and casinos and sizable groves of citrus and avocados, with San Diego County supplying 40% of state production. The Pauma Band of Luiseño Mission Indians and La Jolla Band of Luiseño Indians are a potent force in an ambitious and rich agricultural community in North San Diego County, with Pauma Band Tribal lands totaling some 5,800 acres. Increasingly, fancy suburban housing impinges on agriculture, playing out a perpetual California struggle. In 1985, the Pauma Band began to experiment with agricultural production of its own, planting an initial five acres of Hass avocados, now expanded to nearly sixty acres alongside plantings of Valencia oranges and lemons. The bigger moneymaker is Casino Pauma, opened in May 2001, which makes several nearby Luiseño tribes collectively California's wealthiest.

Orange Groves, Southern California

Seated at a roadside overlook, a woman scans the landscape of orange groves below, in a promotional photograph of the sort spread far and wide by the Southern Pacific Railroad, which owned a sizable acreage in the Southland. By the early 1900s, California crops had serious fans, not just among owner-growers, but as tourists and neighbors recognized hugely satisfying agricultural landscapes. "Picking an orange from a living tree" was a hope voiced by many a train traveler headed for a long sojourn in California. Cities like Riverside and Pasadena, Monrovia and Upland, Highgrove and Citrus Heights were among many where homes and resort hotels built on hilltops offered timeless views. Few crops so excited visitors as oranges (whether Valencias or Navels or the remaining Mission oranges).

Distilling the uniqueness of California into a powerful living symbol, oranges were considered a crop for genteel growers, perhaps even an undertaking suited for amateur hobby farmers. The language attached to small orange groves in Southern California, trimmed and subdivided and planted into parcels of five, ten, twenty, or even thirty acres, was vainglorious. "Oranges for wealth, California for health," boasted one of the thousands of orange crate labels sent around the United States (and abroad).

Orange Groves, Southern California, ca. 1907. Panorama print. Pillsbury Picture Company.

"Sobre Vista," Vineyard of Col. Geo. F. Hooper, on the Eastern
Slope of the Sonoma Mountain

Vineyards nearly rivaled orange groves as a crop responsive
to wise tending and caring ownership. While oranges more
commonly were the moneymaker, vineyards offered a crop,
and a lifestyle, that was as much Old World aristocratic as
aspirationally Mediterranean. Sizable vineyards, often with
field blends of diverse grapes, created a varied landscape,
as growers tried to find what grape grew best where.
Curiously, the Zinfandel grape, a relatively early arrival, had
origins so shrouded in doubt that not until the 1990s did
Carol Meredith, a professor on enology at UC Davis, trace
the variety's origins to Crljenak Kaštelanski and Tribidrag
grapes native to Croatia. Ampelographers, who specialize in
the identification and taxonomy of grapevine origins, were
delighted. Sonoma County is seen in this 1880s view from
Sonoma Mountain, with an early-stage planting in evidence.

"Sobre Vista," Vineyard of Col. Geo. F. Hooper, on the Eastern Slope of the Sonoma Mountain, ca. 1880s. Carleton
Watkins Albumen print. From the album *Photographic Views of El Verano and Vicinity, Sonoma Valley, California.*

BANC PIC 1974.019:123—ALB

Oak-dotted Rangelands Shoulder-to-Shoulder with Luxury Homes, San Benito County near San Juan Bautista, 2006, Peter Goin.

Oak-dotted Rangelands Shoulder-to-Shoulder with Luxury Homes,
San Benito County near San Juan Bautista

Through much of California's history, the principal cash value
of rangeland was as habitat where cattle, sheep, goats, and
other livestock could graze on extensive acreage, sharing
the range with wildlife. As populations in the last thirty years
began growing in areas such as San Benito County, near
Mission San Juan Bautista, homes on the range became
ever more common, and livestock less so. Agriculture and
urbanization are often seen as being at odds, and not in
California alone; among the difficulties of the twenty-first
century is encouraging a return to urban agriculture.

Hetch Hetchy 62" Line, San Joaquin Division, 3 ½ Miles Above Knight's Ferry, Stroupe & Schreiner.

Gelatin silver print. Transferred from the George Blowers writings collection.

BANC PIC 1983.098—PIC

New Large House in the Cornfield, San Joaquin County, 2008, Peter Goin.

Hetch Hetchy 62" Line, San Joaquin Division, 3 ½ Miles Above Knight's Ferry

Aqueducts, canals, flumes, and pipelines are only a few of the distribution systems for water. All must be built, however, and have to be maintained at considerable effort and cost. And the relationship is difficult between urban consumers and users of agricultural water. Agricultural use once consumed ninety percent of the water impounded in California (down now to some seventy percent). Drought cycles of two, five, or even more years do not make the relationship between urban and agricultural water users any more peaceable. In 1919 work began on a controversial dam in Hetch Hetchy Valley, nearly a twin of the Yosemite Valley, just to the north and also within the National Park. Water from O'Shaughnessy Dam, piped through siphons and pipelines to Alameda County, eventually reached 160 miles west to San Francisco. Although the dam was complete in 1923, no deliveries of Tuolumne River water came until 1934. For a time, surplus water actually went to local crops, until the nearly two million customers (2.4 million today) actually needed all the water they could get. The Pulgas Water Temple in Woodside was built to commemorate completion of the delivery system, and today that remains a tranquil destination, seemingly remote from the pipeline assembled to deliver Tuolumne River water to distant reservoirs and gravel infiltration beds in Livermore and Sunol, where water could be stored with a minimum of evaporation and later pumped free. That all cost money, and lots of public investment.

New Large House in the Cornfield, San Joaquin County

Farmhouses in California once were announced by long esplanades of palms, poplars, or other ceremonial trees, with a modest house at road's end. And "modesty" was a seeming by-word of the rural house form and culture. That style is no longer popular, and instead an ambitious ranch-style house—more square feet, more bathrooms, more shelter for pricey farm machinery—is deposited at the center of a field, with corn rows aimed at its midsection. The McMansion or "starter castle," as these grand abodes are sometimes called, is as much an investment in what the social economist Thorstein Veblen called "conspicuous display" as are laser-straight field rows and uniform crops.

Trucks in Front of Spreckles... Field Workers Harvesting Sugar Beets... Clam Shell Dredger Unloading Sugar Beets

The Dyer household (father E.H., and son E.F.) claimed for their family the title of "founders of the American beet sugar industry." From modest beginnings, they launched a dynasty extending to Hawaii, Idaho, Utah, which would land resoundingly in the San Joaquin Valley and other California locations. While for the nineteenth century it was sugar cane—largely sourced from Hawaii—that provided much of the raw sugar, this would change as labor in the Islands grew more difficult to come by and new techniques were developed for cultivating, harvesting, and most important, processing sugar beets. That last item—processing—was the industry's most difficult task, involving a great deal of transportation and even more sophisticated chemistry, to crack sugar from the recalcitrant roots, which can be up to 20% sucrose. The products were not limited to refined sugar—co-products include dried beet pulp and beet molasses, each used in animals feed and in fermentation. The Spreckels family of Monterey County was a competitor, and these operations tended to run large and with lots of capital invested. DYER SCRAPBOOK, written by E.F. Dyer, about 1915 (Call number: 91/110c v. 1).

Trucks in Front of Spreckles Sugar Plant, George Blowers.

Gelatin silver print. Transferred from the George Blowers writings.

Field Workers Harvesting Sugar Beets, George Blowers.

Gelatin silver print. Transferred from the George Blowers writings.

***Clam Shell Dredger Unloading Sugar Beets from Barges on the
Sacramento River, San Joaquin City.*** George Blowers. Gelatin silver print.

Transferred from the George Blowers writings.

BANC PIC 1983.098—PIC folder 2 and 2w

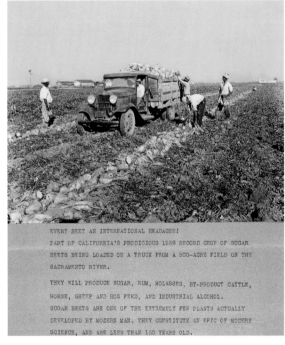

EVERY BEET AN INTERNATIONAL HEADACHE!
PART OF CALIFORNIA'S PRODIGIOUS 1938 RECORD CROP OF SUGAR
BEETS BEING LOADED ON A TRUCK FROM A 500-ACRE FIELD ON THE
SACRAMENTO RIVER.

THEY WILL PRODUCE SUGAR, RUM, MOLASSES, BY-PRODUCT CATTLE,
HORSE, SHEEP AND HOG FEED, AND INDUSTRIAL ALCOHOL.
SUGAR BEETS ARE ONE OF THE EXTREMELY FEW PLANTS ACTUALLY
DEVELOPED BY MODERN MAN. THEY CONSTITUTE AN EPIC OF MODERN
SCIENCE, AND ARE LESS THAN 150 YEARS OLD.

UNLOADING SUGAR BEETS FROM BARGES ON THE SACRAMENTO RIVER.

Alfalfa—C. French Farm

Pride of place, more than 100 years ago, is evident in the farmer's gesture, which emphasizes just how much the Glenn County crop has grown. The crop is alfalfa, a sophisticated protein-dense livestock feed that has traveled the world from Near East to North Island, New Zealand. A hay crop is cut with a mechanical swather, allowed to dry in-place, rolled into windrows, and then further processed for storage. Baling is the most commonly seen storage, with alfalfa formed into stout rectangular or round units where the leafy legume holds its nutritive value for months on end, until a bale is broken up and fed. But alfalfa can be formed into pellets for livestock feed, or chopped as silage into long white tubes, a dozen feet high or twice that.

The End of the Compost Row, Monterey Mushrooms, Morgan Hill

It looks like a vast pile of muck, with a nasty wet pool accumulated at its base. But quite the contrary, this is the sophisticated start of mushroom cultivation. *Agaricus campestris* is just one of the cultivated mushrooms, although as the "button" variety it is known to more Americans than any other. Once composting is completed, button mushroom production is in deep darkness, which keeps the results white and distinctive. For obvious reasons, most mushrooms are grown within easy travel distance of horse racing tracks and large stables, with large manure supplies.

Alfalfa—C. French Farm; five times a year, in Glenn County, breast-high alfalfa is moved by the ranchmen, yielding fat profits with which to buy the coveted luxuries of life, ca. 1915, Charles B. Turrill. Gelatin silver print. Photographs of San Francisco, Yosemite Valley and other scenic California locations. Edna M. Parratt Memorial Fund.

BANC PIC 2011.020:1—PIC

The End of the Compost Row, Monterey Mushrooms, Morgan Hill, 2006, Peter Goin.

A California Bee Ranch: Hunting Wild Bees and Bee Culture

Bees and honey are two momentous crops not because they're enormously profitable, but because without bees, current-day big ticket crops like almonds—a $7 billion earner and California's #2 crop out the farm gate in 2014—would not exist. Harper's Weekly published this broadside in 1881, showing a bewitching variety of honey harvest related activities. The engraving includes an apiary in Santa Rosa, California, which supported Sonoma County's then boundless apple orchards, and the inventive cultivars developed by agronomists and plant breeders such as the renowned Luther Burbank.

Bees in Cherry Orchard, Blossoms, Santa Clara Valley

The pollinators are essential and bees in huge numbers are needed to pollinate almonds. Without bees, California's second total value crop would cease—and that has spawned concern because what is known as colony collapse disorder, with causes still controversial, has killed off the residents of literally hundreds of thousands of hives. The honeybee is not the only pollinator in California, but it's adaptable, relatively tolerant of varied weather, and the bees themselves are equable and docile. If almonds are the California crop that needs the greatest supply of bees-per-tree, the needs of other field crops, trees, and some vegetables are not far behind. And beekeepers make lots of income from their charges, which are moved in their hives on back roads and Interstate highways from location to location, as flowers come onto trees and field crops.

A California Bee Ranch: Hunting Wild Bees and Bee Culture, from *Harper's Weekly*, 1881. Engraving on paper. Robert B. Honeyman, Jr. Collection of Early Californian and Western American Pictorial Material.

Bees in Cherry Orchard, Blossoms, Santa Clara Valley, Peter Goin.

BANC DIG 2017.14:Ag00582

[*Men Milking Sheep*]

The story just about tells itself, from the Frank Adams collection of agricultural themes. In a corral, men are hand-milking ewes in a view dating from the early 1900s. The photographer traveled the United States from 1914 into the 1930s, documenting change in landscapes including ranches, farms, barns, packing houses, and the always-formidable Spreckels Sugar Company, then headquartered in the Salinas Valley, but settled now in Brawley, in the Imperial Valley. The collection is formidable, with forty-two boxes of negatives, many of them lantern slides.

Row of Calves, Bottle-feeding, Johann Dairy, Fresno

Dairies in California often are maintained at a vastly greater size than those in Vermont or Wisconsin or even some of the cherished organic milk and cheese producers such as Straus Dairy, in Marin and Sonoma counties. Johann Dairy in Fresno isn't the largest of the large, in scale and overall production, but it is a carefully managed operation that provides large huts, outdoor space, and pen-to-pen bottle service for dairy-calf rearing. The family operation, still of notable size, is widely respected for providing a particularly benevolent early upbringing for calves.

[*Men Milking Sheep*]. Frank Adams. Lantern slide. California Agriculture Photographs.

BANC PIC 1959.085 LAN Box 10 (#165)

Row of Calves, Bottle-feeding, Johann Dairy, Fresno, 2006, Peter Goin.

BANC DIG 2017.14:Ag00475

Organic Cereal Boxes, Monterey Market, Berkeley
Ingredients in the 1970s, and certainly by the 1980s, might be described as "natural." Turns out the word meant essentially nothing to the USDA and the Food and Drug Administration; it was a placeholder term meant to boost purchaser confidence while administrators farther up the food production ladder struggled to find meaningful language. "Organic" was a subsequent term, and one still used today with some enthusiasm—and confusion. Some states, California among them, set out to define "organic," creating the designation "certified organic"—not just for processed products, but also for beef, grain feeds, and vegetable produce. That too proved wanting, notably for potential purchasers who wanted assurance that what they were eating wasn't laced with pesticides or inorganic fertilizers. In the decades since, academic departments formed around "food studies," and just how to define what's organic (and presumably better for you) is unsettled. How, then, to choose your food—or what goes into the mouths of your children? In this panorama of organic cereal boxes, gleaned at Monterey Market in north Berkeley, the choices are legion. In an age of food sensitivities and allergies and preferences (gluten-free, vegan, lacto-ovo-vegetarian, low carbohydrate), it's best to bring good reading glasses or, for that matter, a magnifying loupe to decipher the fine print. They're there for the discerning to purchase; settling on the correct definition is another matter—and complicated.

Organic Cereal Boxes, Monterey Market, Berkeley, 2007, Peter Goin.

BANC DIG 2017.14:Ag00911-Ag00921_panel

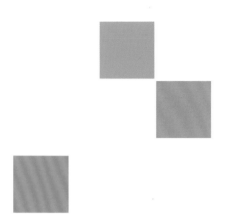

PRODUCTION

THE AGRICULTURAL LANDSCAPE—AND ITS HUMAN DEPENDENTS—AMOUNT TO A LIVING, BREATHING FEATURE OF CALIFORNIA LIFE. Lambs and kids and calves and broilers and turkeys are born, sometimes as heritage breeds, often using upbred hybrid lines. Fruit trees are transplanted and tended, and as with kiwifruit and vineyards, will graft scion and stock into an improved new "whole." (Grafting varieties and alternatives? There's the cleft graft; a bark graft; a side-veneer graft; a splice graft; a whip-and-tongue graft; a bridge graft; an inarch graft, for a start.) Field crops are selected and seeded—open-pollinated, heirloom, heritage, organic, rare seeds, or hybrid. Irrigation may come from canal, ditch, pipeline, or *acequia*, from overhead sprinkler,

siphon, drip emitter, field-flooding, gated pipe, subsurface line, linear-move or center pivot system. The word production invokes every part of animal or crop life: genetics, selection, husbandry, hybridizing for vigor and yield and variety, harvest and curing and commodifying.

Obviously, there is many a backstory: Photographs, whether today or long ago, show the human role in creating a more diverse life of food as human capital.

Production and processing are inelegant sounding words for the careful yet hard work done by agricultural labor providers, growers, entrepreneurs, and food scientists. There are so many contributors to "production"—the owner-growers, the field-bosses and ranch managers, the workers who steer the irrigation waters and later complete a harvest, the dispersed packing houses where the products of the fields and rangelands—literally, the produce—are prepared, arranged, and sent to distributors who ship, or deliver, food raw materials. So much of this is regional or local; a national commodity-support program is in California more imposition than improvisation. Periodically, the United States Congress turns its attention to the so-called "Farm Bill," and battles are launched over what crops and industries, staples, safety, and seed saving, will receive funding. That is no small matter, given epic lobbying by commodity support groups that are an inevitable byproduct of the flourishing world of agribusiness and international trade in foodstuffs. If the benefits of commercialization are sometimes great, the losses can be, too. According to the California Avocado Commission, there are "hundreds of varieties of avocados"—an estimate that the University of California Division of Agriculture & Natural Resources corrects, noting there are more than a thousand named varieties. Only seven are grown commercially in California, and the Hass variety accounts for 95% of the total yearly crop, largely because a coarse outer skin protects the fruit from damage in shipping.

Only the elite produce store will reliably sell the other six, in season: Bacon, Fuerte, Gwen, Pinkerton, Reed, and Zutano varieties. That leaves out most of a thousand more. The contrasts of commercial and hobbyist- or backyard crop production are another story—if a good one.

Animals and cultivars—plants selected by intentional human intervention for desirable characteristics—are the bread and butter of agronomy and higher education study of the business of agriculture. And behind that is an elaborate political economy of research, field study, experimentation, and at times, government support or interdiction, as environmental historian Courtney Fullilove writes in a 2017 book, *The Profit of the Earth: The Global Seeds of American Agriculture*. Has any state so benefited as California from U.S. Department of Agriculture and U.S. Patent Office efforts to gather plant varieties from the rounded corners of the world? Doubtful. Ethnobotanists and ethnopharmacologists go abroad to find seeds and cuttings and tubers and drug remedies that might prove useful—and profitable—if they can be adapted and grown. At times, important skills are already imported: Fullilove documents the role of immigrant agricultural knowledge, whose work with plant and animal varieties is still a formidable contributor to agricultural innovation across California. ■

Harvesting Asparagus Panel, 2007, Peter Goin.

including flatlands and even bayside rangeland, provides natural communities and habitat so important for biological diversity. Once shaped by Native American management and regular burning that maintained grasslands or oak-dotted landscapes, these offer a mosaic of uses: grazing, watershed protection, venues for hiking, picnicking, family outings. While a formal setting aside of protected space began in earnest in the 1930s, there were earlier attempts, too, and a steady accumulation of acreage means herds of sheep, cattle, and goats grazing public lands are a contrast to the scattered horse ranches and small ranchettes so popular among long-established residents that adjoin designated public space. Sheep work the East Bay Hills, with Oakland in the distance.

Harvesting Asparagus

Asparagus harvesting is done daily for a several-month period, involving a lot of stooped-over labor, experience to guide the sharp harvest knives, and a good sense of how to avoid damaging the crowns underground. Mexican field workers in red and blue are harvesting asparagus. A.M. Farms was founded in 1983 and specializes in grapes, asparagus, and alfalfa, and employs seven people at this location, with additional farm hands brought on during harvesting season. A significant proportion of this farm's high-quality asparagus crop is reserved for international markets. The individual photographs were created in 2007 and assembled onto the panel and printed as an exhibition print in 2008.

Flock of Sheep on the Low Foothills of Oakland

Sheep in profusion, with a city beyond: The marvels of the extended San Francisco Bay Area include a well-connected and actively managed system of greensward or open space. With a total area of 4.5 million acres, this is the largest open space included in any metropolitan area in the United States. In 2018, more than a third of that area is grazed, and all of it provides ecosystem services, which means it is what is often referred to as "working rangeland." The belt of green space around Bay Area cities, generally in the hills but

Flock of Sheep Numbering Several Thousand Head, on the Low Foothills of Oakland with the City in the Background, date unknown, Roberts & Roberts. Gelatin silver print. George Blowers collection.

BANC PIC 1983.098—PIC folder 1

Mexican Farm Workers Harvesting Strawberries,
Monterey County

While farmworkers will bring along small radios and can bundle up when picking strawberries, the work is anything but comfortable. Bent over as they work filling small boxes with the delicate fruit, harvest is hard work, and especially harvesting low-growing crops such as strawberries remains physically taxing agricultural labor, done overwhelmingly by immigrant farm workers from Mexico or elsewhere in Latin America. While strawberries are seen especially often in Monterey County, they grow in many a spot depending on the growth season, and completing the harvest requires multiple passes over several weeks, even with determinate varieties that are supposed to yield much of their fruit in a concentrated period. The same story can be offered for blackberries or raspberries or blueberries, which have a long growing history in the state.

Mexican Farm Workers Harvesting Strawberries,
Monterey County, 2007, Peter Goin.

BANC DIG 2017.14:Ag00356

Workers Pruning Trellises For Wine Grapes; Sightline with Foster Farms Chicken Feed Plant in Distance, 2006, Peter Goin.

Young Man Posing in a Red Sweater with Bin Full of Artichokes, 2007, Peter Goin.

Antonio Perez Weighing Asparagus at A.M. Farms, near Stockton. 2007, Peter Goin.

BANC DIG 2017.14:Ag00789

Workers Pruning Trellises For Wine Grapes; Sightline with Foster Farms Chicken Feed Plant in Distance

"Revolutionary grape-pruners," might describe the montage, though backed by a huge feed mill in the distance, in an ensemble that not for the first time was reminiscent of the contrasts of pastoral and industrial in German expressionist films of the 1930s. The bandana-protected pruners so assiduously shaping the trellised grape vines work under the looming presence of a Fritz Lang-styled industrial plant.

Young Man Posing in a Red Sweater with Bin Full of Artichokes

A young artichoke harvester stands braced against the weight of the full canasta of artichokes on his back during the March peak of harvest near Castroville, Monterey County. While the scale and intensiveness of agriculture in California brings sizable profit margins, with that comes prodigious expenses. The machinery and labor requirements required to sustain this artichoke-harvesting crew near Watsonville is nothing a small-scale operator could undertake. And artichokes—like asparagus, cruciferous vegetables, and a number of other crops—need several passes of harvesters, not just one, since the crop matures at varying rates and it is wasteful to leave produce in the field.

Antonio Perez Weighing Asparagus at A.M. Farm

If cultivation of soil, planting, fertilizing, and irrigating are essential to the crop-production cycle, those each represent grower investments rather than cash producers. It is harvest, processing, and packing that turn a crop from potential to income. The common link is, unsurprisingly, the steady and savvy addition of labor, much in evidence in these two photographs. Asparagus is a crop that in California is generally found in the Sacramento—San Joaquin Delta. A fast-growing perennial grown in deep fertile soils, the crowns produce "grass" from spring to early summer that, for best results, must be packed and processed carefully. The crates and boxes often used for shipment are singular—wide where the base of the asparagus spears are nestled; much narrower at the top, where the tips stick up: crate labels for asparagus are particularly sought after by collectors.

Chinese Drying Grapes, 1890–1900. Gelatin silver Print. Miscellaneous California Views.

BANC PIC 1905.12798—PIC

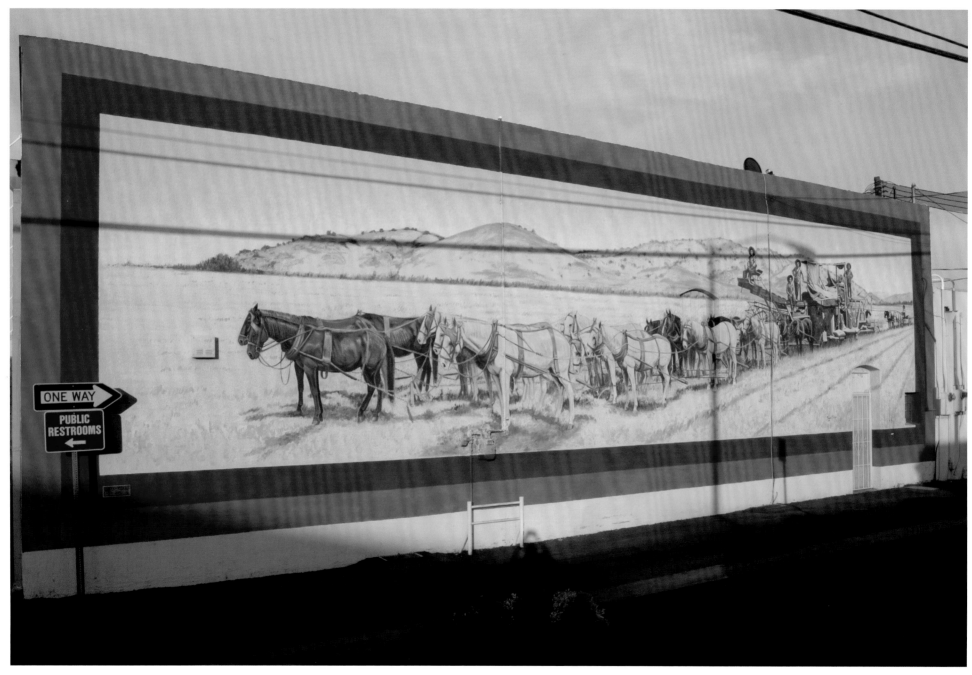

One of Sixteen Murals in Exeter, California, 2007, Peter Goin.

Chinese Drying Grapes

A dozen workers tend drying raisin grapes as a part of commercial fruit preparation for sale. If fresh fruits and vegetables are a kind of culinary ideal, even in California availability becomes a tussle when the days grow short and temperatures cool—much cannot be grown in greenhouses. And choices in the past were far less than today: Before there was refrigeration and readily available long-distance transport, the keys to safe food storage involved varied kinds of curing. Vegetables and fruits could be preserved using techniques that are coming back into popularity these days, such as fermentation, smoking, or pickling. Also possible was canning, once the glass canning jar invented in 1858 by John Landis Mason entered widespread use, thanks to commercialization by Ball, Kerr, and other firms. The grandmother of all preservation techniques, which works well even for meat, is desiccation or drying. In Spanish-Mexican California, charqui (from the Quechua word *ch'arki*) was a favored means of preserving meat, and what we now call "jerky" owes much to the power of the past; pemmican and fish-drying have their own distinguished curing histories. Drying is a great asset in saving fruits and vegetables for later use: Removing water (sometimes by applying salt, sometimes by freeze-drying, sometimes with sun or heat), can prevent spoilage, reduce weight, and make transport far easier. Fruit, especially, is dried and sold. Once it was widely treated with sulfur dioxide to preserve color and reduce bacterial growth, though less so now. Careful inspection of any grocery store will reveal racks or bulk bins of dried apricots, apples, pears, plums, bananas—or dried chilies, mushrooms, corn, zucchini, beans, onion, and a thousand additional spices. For California, it was especially fruit that was dried, and while huge dehydrators and natural gas or biomass are used now, in nineteenth century California and through the 1960s, crops once harvested would be laid out in shallow trays in the summer sun. And a favorite, inevitably, was the dried grape—the raisin—once a lunchbox standard, and even now a regular addition to curries, oatmeal, dry cereals and muesli, and many another recipe.

Loading Native Hay—G.H. Atkins Ranch near Placerville, California, ca. 1915, Charles B. Turrill. Gelatin silver print. Charles B. Turrill photographs of San Francisco, Yosemite Valley and other scenic California locations.

One of Sixteen Murals in Exeter

While the area in wheat and other grains in California pales compared to field crop acreage in the Great Plains and even the Midwest, once upon a time Sacramento Valley wheat was prodigious and had worldwide fame. Grain raising was so profitable that giant harvesters, hauled by up to a couple of dozen stout draft animals, were needed for harvest. A pivotal figure in the California grain industry was Dr. Hugh Glenn. A Civil War veteran, he came across the plains and worked a claim on Murderer's Bar for a few months until he found truth in the adage "It takes a mine to run a mine," sold out, and began hauling freight to the mining camps. There, there was income. He did what various forty-niners would do, returning to the East several times, but with an eye toward a future home in California. He brought his family west, acquired 45,000 acres of land outright, and at one point claimed to have 80,000 acres seeded in grain, which earned him a reputation in the 1870s as the Wheat King of California. Some of his acreage came from the heirs of U.S.

Consul Thomas Larkin, and with that, Glenn became one of the largest landowners in California and Nevada. Not given to small ventures, he bought livestock, too, building a fortune on wheat and meat. Eventually he sold his livestock operation for $250,000 to Miller & Lux, who were in the process of accumulating their own vast holdings. Dr. Glenn met an untimely end: murdered in 1883 by a disgruntled ranch hand. Nonetheless, his role in making an agricultural stronghold of the northern Sacramento Valley led to Glenn County being split off and named for him in 1891. Murals commemorating California Wheat laud a now-bygone era. Pride of place is important in California agriculture, and cities and towns will commemorate founders and other important figures in local history. There are, as of this writing, sixteen murals throughout the downtown area of Exeter. This mural is titled "Golden Harvest," number 13, by Claudia Fletcher.

Loading Native Hay

"Haying" is perhaps the perfect farm family activity—much in evidence here, with patient horses trained to pull the wagon, adults pitch-forking the cured hay onto the flatbed, and three young children posing for the photographer, hunkered down in the field. In the middle distance is an orchard of fruit trees, and beyond that oak trees. Hay is a cured grass-like product, cut by scythe or swather, dried in windrows, and then gathered. Native hay provides nutritious feed; the varieties of planted and cultivated grass are many, and alfalfa has higher food value for livestock, but greater production costs.

Labor in support of California agriculture is a perpetual need; during the 1930s and 1940s, migrants leaving the Dust Bowl provided a labor supply that was readily and often ruthlessly exploited, but that began to wane by World War II. Afterward, more and more labor in California came from across the southern border with Mexico. Growers and the developing industrial agriculture and agribusiness interests in California grew concerned about inroads made by organized labor, and reports issued about groups such as the Industrial Workers of the World (IWW, or Wobblies), which began with workers mining gold, silver, and copper in western states, but gradually moved to organize laborers in farming and, in a remarkable episode, among cowboys working on cattle ranches. This typescript report was a first effort to assess the role of the IWW in California agriculture; of course, efforts would reach into the Hispanic/Chicano/Latina(o) community with Cesar Chavez and Dolores Huerta leading efforts from the late 1960s onward with the United Farm Workers. BANC m F862.6 F348.

[Federal Writers' Project. Oakland, Calif. 1939]
THE INDUSTRIAL WORKERS OF THE WORLD
IN CALIFORNIA AGRICULTURE

Conceived in a welter of industrial conflict, the accouchement of the organization known as the Industrial Workers of the World took place in 1904. It marked a distinct leftward step from the fluttering timidity of the Socialist Party, while the Communist Party, which was destined to carry its basic principles to their ultimate conclusion in their Moscow-buttressed ideology, was then only an European cellar-hidden movement. According to William D. Haywood, General Secretary-Tresurer of the Industrial Workers of the World:[...]

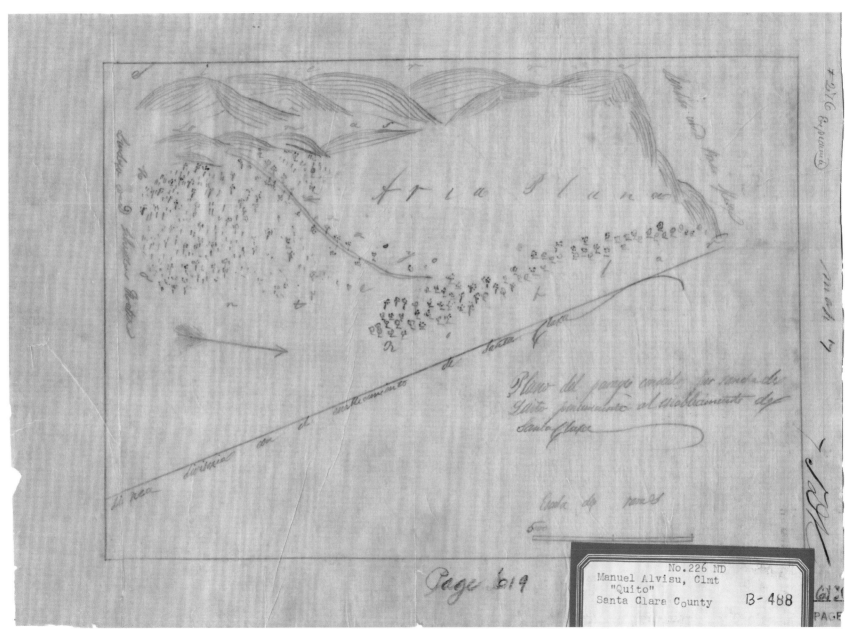

United States. District Court (California: Northern District). *Plano del parage [sic] conscido por Rancho de Quito,* Land case 226. Oriented with north toward the bottom. Pen and ink map. Land Case map B-488

Plano del parage [sic] conscido por Rancho de Quito...

About 300 land grants were issued during the Spanish–Mexican era in California history, extending from 1769–1848, when the Treaty of Guadalupe Hidalgo ended the conflict between the U.S. and Mexico and made California a territory of the United States. Sorting out land ownerships after the Treaty was a hugely complicated legal business: thirty of the grants from the Spanish era had largely gone to communities and missions. But all mission lands except for a few church-specific sites were secularized by the Mexican government in 1834, many broken up and redistributed. The remaining 270 Mexican-era grants went largely to individuals, and those mostly came in the last few years of Mexican control of California, in an attempt to parry the claims of immigrants arriving in Alta California with designs on land acquisition. The great complication after the Treaty was sorting out who owned what. The U.S. Congress created a Board of California Land Commissioners that was supposed to follow the Treaty by accepting preexisting claims. Instead, grantees were required to prove ownership and document their holdings with maps showing exact boundaries. These maps—known as *diseños*—typically were more rustic than precise, following metes and bounds surveying, which defined boundaries by physical features: an oak tree here, a rock outcrop there, a fencepost, a promontory, a creek that could easily change course. Court cases resulted, and the collective archive of court records for the federal Northern District cases reached The Bancroft Library in 1951. Toward the end of the twentieth century, Northern and Southern District cases files, held in portfolios with maps filed separately, were unified in Berkeley. The diseño for Quito Rancho Alviso, in the Santa Clara Valley, is typical enough of the maps presented by petitioners to the Board, and it sought clear title for the Alviso family, whose original

members came to Mission Santa Clara in the late eighteenth century. Domingo Alviso served as a corporal with the De Anza expedition. After a brief period of ownership by José Noriega, in 1844 ownership of Rancho Quito went to Alviso's son Ignacio, who filed the required legal petitions for Rancho Rincon de los Esteros (now the San Jose Airport) and Rancho Quito, then used largely for livestock grazing. But resolution was slow: squatters occupied significant parts of the ranchos, contested title, and with legal fees and debts once-sizable landholdings were with time were whittled away or sold to covetous Americans. Farming of small parcels replaced grazing sheep and cattle, and in 1874 came changes to fence laws, which in a reversal required livestock owners to fence their properties so animals could not impinge on croplands.

Olive Picking on the Quito Ranch, Alice Iola Hare, Gelatin silver print. Alice Iola Hare Photograph Collection.

BANC PIC 1905.04953—PIC

Olive Picking on the Quito Ranch

Harvest work at the Quito Ranch olive orchards is being done by twenty laborers, all of them to appearances emigrants to California, and likely from China. Olive picking on this scale was labor writ large, and the faces of the workers reflect that toil.

Sorosis Fruit Company's Packing House

The prodigious investment involved in processing produce is a feature of California agriculture much in evidence, ever since the late 1800s. Granted, that had to wait for the development of intricate systems of transportation—and even refrigeration, not widespread until the early 1900s. The Sorosis Fruit Company was just one of the fruit processing and packing giants in the Santa Clara Valley.

Sorosis Fruit Company's Packing House, Alice Iola Hare. Albumen print. Alice Iola Hare Photograph Collection.

BANC PIC 1905:04997—PIC

Laborers Picking Blood Oranges... Picking Pears in Orchard

In some respects, agricultural labor is not much changed. On the left are workers on tall ladders harvesting oranges near Exeter, in the San Joaquin Valley; on the right crates of pears, picked and sorted in the Santa Clara Valley, once the epicenter for California fruit growing. Clambering into trees or mounting ladders makes for a rugged and difficult day, and large sacks of oranges or other fruit are heavy, awkward, and must be handled with delicacy, lest the cargo be bruised or otherwise damaged. Fruit growing in each of these areas brings risks: For Exeter and Porterville, which became the citrus center once housing began to dominate the Inland Empire of Southern California, every few years brings the risk of hard freezes that can damage ripe fruit stored on the trees until growers decide the market price is high enough for harvest to proceed. And the Santa Clara Valley—once home to a seeming sea of apricots, peaches, apples and pears, plums and prunes and other tree crops and truck farms— began to suburbanize in the 1930s and '40s, and by World War II, fruit growers were cashing out to move elsewhere or retire from the business. With groves giving way to housing and highways, change was afoot, and yet another turnaround would come in the 1980s as Silicon Valley firmed up and created huge campuses for their workers. Names on the land are among the few signs of what used to be there, along with carefully assembled books chronicling the legacy of ranchos, fruit groves, electric interurban railroads, the packing houses, and the shipping piers and stark worker housing that once shaped a signature landscape.

Laborers Picking Blood Oranges (near Exeter, Tulare County), 2006, Peter Goin.

Picking Pears in Orchard of A. Block, Santa Clara Valley, California, 1900–1910, Alice Iola Hare. Gelatin silver print. Alice Iola Hare Photograph Collection.

BANC PIC 1905:04984—PIC

The Cutting Room

Campbell, California, was once home to a variety of packing plants, established to streamline processing of fruit arriving from orchards and groves in San Mateo and Santa Clara counties. Among the most substantial enterprises was the plant owned by George Hyde & Company, seen here between 1915 and 1921. It was one big enterprise, with a cannery, a grading area, a packing house for whole fruit, a day care center, a crate-making operation, and a sizable fruit drying facility. The Hyde & Company operation was acquired from an earlier owner in Campbell, and while the George E. Hyde & Co. Canning Operation held together for a time, it would later go into other ownership. Often, as here, it was women who handled the sorting and grading of fruit. There is even a wiki titled "Packing Houses of Santa Clara Valley" that tracks the history of packing houses and fruit producers.

Flowing like digital data

A twenty-first century packing house is a highly specialized and technologically sophisticated operation, evident in this view of the Exeter—Ivanhoe Citrus Sunkist Packing House. The fruit are literally digital oranges—lined up for initial grading by electronic sensors. Size, weight, and a quality review for color and imperfections on each individual orange happens at high speed as oranges are measured and their data recorded. Next, the fruit is routed to the appropriate hand-grading lines for refined sorting and evaluation by workers. Blue nitrile or cotton gloves are often in evidence, guarding fruit rinds against chance damage in handling, and protecting workers from oils that can cause sun sensitivity and even blistering of human hands.

The Cutting Room, 1920.

BANC PIC 1982.069:25—ALB

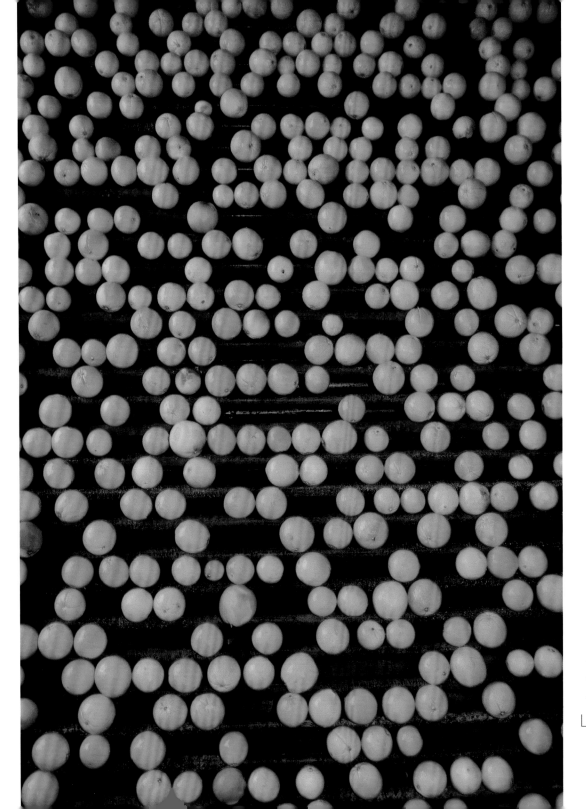

Flowing like digital data, these fruit emerge from a second wash and head toward electronic sorting in the Exeter–Ivanhoe Citrus Sunkist packing house, 2006, Peter Goin.

BANC DIG 2017.14:Ag00543

Buena Vista Vineyard, Sonoma—Plowing. Albumen stereograph, all from **Vintage in California,** Bradley & Rulofson, Publishers. Stereographs of the West from The Bancroft Library Pictorial Collection. Eadweard J. Muybridge [all four stereographs] BANC PIC 1988.103:3—STER; **Buena Vista Vineyard, Sonoma–Grape Cutting**; BANC PIC 1988.103:3—STER; **Buena Vista Vineyard, Sonoma–The Cooper Shop**; BANC PIC 1988.103:16—STER; **Buena Vista Vineyard, Sonoma—Crushing the Grape**; BANC PIC 1988.103:6—STER

California hills, vineyards, and that tourist imperative: parking, Chimney Rock winery, Stags Leap District, Napa Valley, 2007, Peter Goin.

BANC DIG 2017.14:Ag00849

Buena Vista Vineyard, Sonoma—Four Stereographs

These stereographs bring together two legends: famed photographer Eadweard Muybridge, whose nineteenth century studies established an early standard for photography as a tool of scientific inquiry and stop-motion studies, and the Buena Vista Vineyard, California's oldest winery, founded by Agoston Haraszthy in 1857. Buena Vista, still extant today, established Sonoma County as a viable viticultural site, and the Hungarian-born Haraszthy was its prophet and promoter, although his initial enthusiasm far exceeded his budget, forcing him to solicit outside funding from sources including San Francisco banker William Ralston. A relentless traveler and agricultural innovator, Haraszthy is credited with introducing hundreds of grape varieties to California—some of which he test-planted in Wisconsin, before continuing west. While the Buena Vista operation would be laid low more than once by financial straits and by the grape pest phylloxera, it was never entirely abandoned. In fact, by the 1940s, it was undergoing the sorts of ownership changes so typical of wineries in Napa, Sonoma, and Marin counties, with deep-pocket buyers from the business world acquiring vineyards estates where they could serve as patrons, hosting friends and visitors. Rarely would they recuperate more than a fraction of their financial investment, but the payoff would come in sociability and an investment that imitated the premier cru estates of France. Muybridge created a series of images marking distinct phases of the wine-making process: cultivation, harvest, the grape crush, and coopers at work forming barrels to hold wine, as it formed up.

Agoston Haraszthy, The Haraszthy Family: San Francisco, California, July 1, 1886, Manuscript, BANC MSS C-D 418; Hubert Howe Bancroft collection …[A]t his own expense in 1861, [Haraszthy] went to Europe and returned with a collection of Two Hundred Thousand Cuttings and Rooted vines embraced in a catalog of Four Hundred and Eighty-seven names… The Legislature declining to receive the imported vines at their cost, part of them were planted on his Buena Vista property and the balance sold to private individuals throughout the State for the first time causing a general and large plantation of foreign vines in every direction. Col. Haraszthy continued his viticultural labors up to the time of his death in Nicaragua in July 1869. And it may be justly said that though many were the workers in the early days of this pursuit, none worked with as much enthusiasm, harder, with more telling effect, or as disinterestedly for the promotion of Viticulture as did Col. Agoston Haraszthy. To him more than to any one else is due its rarified extension and he may well be called and he often has been, the Father of the Vine in California.

California hills, vineyards, and that tourist imperative

Since gaining fame at the "Judgment of Paris" of 1976, Napa has been a destination for hordes of tourists, enamored of vineyards, architecture of out-scale proportions, with budgets to match, who bring with them a thirst for wine and scenery. Wineries that can afford it meet that need, and create landscapes of the grape that play to local advantages, as here at the Chimney Rock Winery in the Stags Leap District. A hundred years ago, Napa and Sonoma counties accounted for over 70% of the vineyards in California. Now, there is a great deal of competition, and prime bottom-land is valued at over $140,000 an acre in the most valued Napa sites, a price that is, as a rule, more usually found only in peak value urban property. Instead, vineyards like this one along Napa's Silverado Trail ascend the hillsides, not just because of land cost, but also to chase terroir—a concept linking site and specific viticultural qualities embraced by only some of California's wineries. It is asphalt and suburban castles that stake the best claim to the fertile ground, but the winery nonetheless memorializes the scene on many of their wine labels.

Grafted grapevines in field, Mercier Grapevines

Tree and vine crops in lands of Mediterranean-type (summer-dry) climate including Spain, Greece, Italy, Portugal, southern France, and North Africa have since Antiquity been singled-out and lauded as examples of "a permanent agriculture," in the timeless phrase of the geographer J. Russell Smith. But permanence earns little face-time with commercial-scale growers in California, where changing fashions and agricultural profit-seeking compel quick alterations matched to fleeting fashions in food or, in this case, wine. At this sophisticated facility in Pleasants Valley, near the fertile Putah Creek Fan, a French firm maintains a high-end greenhouse where grape vines are selected and grafted to provide rootstock for growers who choose surprisingly often in northern California to tear out existing vineyards that could have another hundred years of useful life and replace them with different clones of the same grape variety—or go to entirely different varieties. Only the most sanguine (and established) of agricultural producers is willing to stay with old vines that may produce far less as they age. For the youthful—and competitive—change often awaits, although there are wineries where the star products proudly proclaim "Old Vine" below the varietal name on the label.

*Grafted grapevines in field, **Mercier Grapevines**, 2007, Peter Goin.*

BANC DIG 2017.14:Ag00879a

AGRI-ENVIRONMENT

IN EVEN A CASUAL VISIT WITH A CALIFORNIA FARMER OR RANCHER OR AGRONOMIST OR FARM-TO-TABLE PARTISAN, the environment is inevitably a topic. A city dweller, plunked down in a rural setting, might wonder if such talk isn't at an uncomfortable risk of salting an open wound. But conversations usually take a distinct and a predictable turn. The agriculturalist, in seeming defiance of all odds, will voice strong sentiment in favor of protecting the environment: "Every day of my life I'm an environmentalist. Look at where my family and I live and where we work—How could we do anything that would be bad for this place?" If growing crops and raising animals for the public is your life and livelihood, it makes sense that creating a substandard product that harms the environment or risks poisoning the public at large is nonsensical. Producers care. They want us to understand that they work hard to keep things clean, orderly, attractive, and ultimately, sustainable.

An example helps. In 2012 the novelist Alice Walker, a resident of Mendocino County for the last 25 years or so, wrote *The Chicken Chronicles*. During an interview about the book, journalist Meredith May remarks that Walker has for years raised a thoroughly diversified flock of chickens for their eggs. May asks Walker what she makes of the burgeoning backyard-chicken movement in the greater San Francisco Bay Area. Walker's response is characteristically direct and voices a widely-held perception: "People want to eat eggs that are not poisonous. They want to eat chicken that hasn't been tortured. They want to reconnect with a way of life that's so much more agreeable to humanity than what we've endured for the last 50 years with factory farming." Those are all good points.

The language of food security, preservation and production, even harm and health is no vocabulary of absolutes. Safe food, public awareness, and the adjustment of agricultural activities to conform with regulatory facts such as clean water and endangered species protection are subjects of debate. One ringing reality rules them all: Evaluating, acquiring, and eating food—along with wearing clothes fashioned from cotton, or linen, leather, wool, or other products raised in nature—is a necessary everyday act that goes far back into human prehistory. As Peter Kareiva, an ecologist and Chief Scientist at The Nature Conservancy puts it, "We're in nature. The deal is how to work with it, and how to help it work for us. The better we are at ensuring that people get nature's benefits, the better we'll be doing at conservation." Pleasingly, nature is less fragile than people tend to think. But agriculture changes the land. A landscape will never be "pristine" and it likely never was. Beyond that, we need to adapt to what is acceptable, and be able to explain why it is so.

City people are surprised by this. If they think about farming and agriculture at all (and more are), the thoughts burble with concern about pesticides, potential soil fertility loss, food quality, and precious water flowing wastefully onto fields. The farmer's reply is that cities are a force of change themselves, and rarely arise to the benefit of nature. By official count, urban dwellers make up 98% of the human population of California. This creates a separation of attitude and awareness between producers and consumers of food. Ultimately, livestock producers and crop growers have an audience to keep happy and satisfied, a constituency that lives in cities, towns, and suburbs. And, furthermore, those more densely occupied places have for decades swelled California, taking up land on the urban fringe.

Agri-World, Madera County, 2010, Peter Goin.

Agri-World, Madera County

While in some views a universe unto itself, California's "Agri-World" is shaped by a disproportionately urban population. Even today, growers and many ag workers live in towns and cities, commuting to work, as here on the road to Yosemite National Park along Highway 146 in Madera County. The American West as a whole still functions as what the historian Walter Prescott Webb called an oasis civilization, with population concentrated in urban and suburban areas, and a scattered rural population—though that is on the increase, particularly in the Sacramento—San Joaquin valleys and along the Central Coast.

Packing Apples at F. Burris' Packing House

With warehouse walls showing the slightly battered appearance of long hard use, safely stored crates of apples are ready for storage and sales. Agriculture can bring in solid income, but many growers spend only when they need to, preferring to keep on the conservative side in terms of capital expenditures. The look of this successful grower is casual and confident, togged out in Levi's jeans. The sizable crop of apples is warehoused in the Santa Clara Valley, at the core of the "Valley of Heart's Delight." Apples in the Santa Clara Valley, in the Pajaro Valley west of Salinas, and in other northern California areas such as Sebastopol, once home base to the exquisite Gravenstein apple, are either abandoned so unpicked windfall apples ferment below the trees, or the Biblical fruit is relegated to the status of backyard crop.

Packing Apples at F. Burris' Packing House, 1900–1910, Alice Iola Hare.
Gelatin Silver Print. Alice Iola Hare Photograph Collection.

BANC PIC 1905:04998—PIC

The Virgin Waterscape, The California Water Atlas

published in 1979 under the auspices of then-Governor Jerry Brown, was created by geographer–cartographer William Bowen and his research team. Aside from sheer beauty, the massive atlas reveals just how much California even forty years ago was a system of plumbing: at the large end, dams and reservoirs and tunnels, aqueducts and canals. "The Virgin Waterscape" is a particularly significant product. An impressive inset map shows the greater San Francisco Bay Area, with areas once regularly flooded by seasonal inundations, and the rest of the map tells the larger but related story of the Sacramento—San Joaquin valleys—some call that assemblage the "Great Central Valley"—where the movement of water in late spring and early summer would inundate large parts of the land. No one can afford to waste water, so the end-user distribution scales down to a conserving overhead sprinkler system or even quarter-inch drip irrigation lines ending in tendrils of one-pint-per-minute emitters. In *Up and Down California in 1860–1864*, the naturalist William Henry Brewer relates in a memoir sights he witnessed in 1862, where by the end of January in the Sierra foothills town of Sonora, "102 inches of water has fallen." He continues, "An old acquaintance, a *buccaro* [vaquero, or buckaroo], came down from a ranch that was overflowed. The floor of their one-story house was six weeks under water before the house went to pieces. The "Lake" was at that point sixty miles wide, from the mountains on one side to the hills on the other. This was in the Sacramento Valley. Steamers ran back over the ranches fourteen miles from the river, carrying stock, etc., to the hills." Observers described the Sutter Buttes with wildlife including such keystone predators as grizzly bears, mountain lions, and wolves retreating into the volcanic peaks to escape floodwaters. Those would not come every year—the El Niño/La Niña cycles portend drought-flood events only at unpredictable intervals.

The Virgin Waterscape

Lake
Estimated natural shorelines.

Freshwater Marsh
Land inundated annually and populated by tules, cattails, or other hydrophytic vegetation.

Riparian Forest
Broadleaf deciduous forest growing naturally on the sides or banks of rivers and streams, and in bottomlands.

Coastal Brackish Marsh
Land inundated alternately by saline water and fresh water.

Coastal Salt Marsh
Land along the upper intertidal zone of protected shallow bays, estuaries and coastal lagoons. Salt tolerant plants predominate.

Saline and Alkaline Lands
Sinks and basin rim lands characterized by intermittent water high in mineral content.

The Virgin Waterscape, The California Water Atlas

BANC REF ff G1526.C3 1979

Unprecedented Floods Sweep West Side: Dam and River

Across California, the control of water sources is a constant and unceasing battle. Today, pro-dam advocates are quick to complain that there have been no new dams contracted since the early 1980s, and there is truth to that. But even dams built a hundred years ago were snarled in lawsuits over whether waters could be diverted, whether long-distance movement through aqueducts was legal. The effects of water diversions and ripping, plowing—and even paving—once oak-dotted and rich valley bottomlands are today evident to any traveler around the state. After a half-decade of drought years from 2012–2017, talk is again wafting through the air about adding 16.5 feet to the height of Shasta Dam, at the head of the federal California Water Project, which might provide a more secure water supply for urban users. That would, rather pointedly in 2018, be a boon as well for the 600,000-acre Westlands Water District, the largest irrigation district in the United States, and a relatively late arrival on the scene and a subject of enduring controversy. Whether the theme is supercharging the capacity of Shasta Dam, or firming up a tunnel delivery system for water ducted underneath the Delta, it is likely that the disputes over where water goes, and to whose benefit, will be many and prodigiously impassioned. Among knowing parties to the debates, everyone will be at least a little bit "right."

Unprecedented Floods Sweep West Side: Dam and River, 1938, Laval.

Gelatin silver print. Agriculture and Flood-Related Photographs from the Miller & Lux Collection.

BANC PIC 1973.056—PIC folder 2

Lincoln Village Maintenance District Water Tower,
San Joaquin County

No theme spawns more persistent environmental controversy
in California than the control and dispensing of water
delivered to a growing city population—or to competing
uses. Agriculture in California is a big water consumer,
although at a rate far lower than 30 years ago, when farms
and agriculture used 90% of impounded surface water.
Water towers such as this one, in San Joaquin County,
represent a balance of urban population, with cleansed
and filtered water supplies, against the weighty demands of
almonds, dairies, orange groves, tomatoes and tomatillos,
chili peppers, and pistachios. Secure water supplies for
residents is an obvious public safety concern, and during
the five-year drought of the 2010s, reports from the eastern
San Joaquin Valley told of residents opening taps and getting
only blowing air, a signal of safe water gone entirely missing.

Lincoln Village Maintenance District Water
Tower, San Joaquin County, 2010, Peter Goin.

Close-up of Changing Tank Nozzles before Spraying Emergent Lettuce, Monterey County, 2007, Peter Goin.

BANC DIG 2017.14:Ag00746

Crop Duster Passing Overhead, Fresno County, 2006, Peter Goin.

BANC 2017.14:Ag00198

Close-up of Changing Tank Nozzles before Spraying Emergent Lettuce, Monterey County

Any family that raises its own lettuce understands that with a crop of leafy greens must come vigilance against snails and slugs and assorted other pests. Growers of commercial—but not organic—crops have means of dealing with unwanted field pests, suggested here near the town of Spreckels, in Monterey County. Lettuce is close to an omnipotent force in California agriculture, especially since the Salinas Valley so dominates production. More than a $2 billion crop, lettuce in all forms says "California." Statewide, treatments may include spraying to reduce any of a variety of pests; in this case, the crop cannot be marketed as organic, although signs on neighboring fields warn applicators against allowing spray to drift into adjoining properties. Some lettuce is organic, though not necessarily just varieties raised by small producers, since "organic" crops are a business that can be worth millions of dollars to current-day California growers.

Crop Duster Passing Overhead, Fresno County

When crop dusters prepare their runs, which can apply everything from airborne rice seed to fertilizer to pesticides and cotton defoliants. The nozzle-check is the essential prelude. The magenta dye cleans out the lines and shows that all wing sprayers are working in concert to produce an even spread at a rough airfield north of the old Tulare Lake Bed, in Kings and Kern counties. There is nothing quite like a soaking with magenta dye to wake you up at mid-morning.

Strawberry Plastic: Field in Preparation, Santa Cruz County

A Santa Cruz field awaits the transplanting of crops. Of course, setting pesticide debates momentarily aside, what is most dramatic in this view is the technology required to shape the planting beds, covering them with tractor-laid plastic, while preparing the ground for a cost-intensive planting. What's being farmed is not an acreage of carefully perforated white plastic, but instead strawberries. And it is strawberries, especially, that pose a problem for California growers: They constitute a nearly $2.3 billion crop (2015), yet only a small acreage is farmed organically. Instead, strawberries have long been subject to soil fumigation to discourage pests including subterranean nematodes, although recent legislation and regulations have forced a change in growing practices. Soil fumigation for strawberries is regarded by non-organic growers and some crop research specialists as a necessary evil. But there is also a sizable opposition, especially because strawberries have a huge audience among small children. Any form of pesticide has to balance cost and public disfavor against diminished crop production and a perhaps lessened visual appeal of organic fruit and vegetables. Dealing with invasive plants and animals is a constant ecological fact. No batch of seeds ready for planting is entirely clean and pure; no dairy cow is guaranteed germ-free; no boat ballast pumped into San Francisco Bay or the Sacramento–San Joaquin Delta is wholly without contaminants or invasive mussels. The first major invasion from Mediterranean Europe came not by intent, but by accident: the vessels of explorers carried not just men (women on board were few) and weapons, they held livestock and food stocks for men and animals—and seeds. California had Mediterranean grasses and invasive weeds aplenty long before it had missions and presidios, and those spread with élan.

Strawberry Plastic: Field in Preparation, Santa Cruz County, 2006, Peter Goin.

Contains No Spinach

While Earthbound Farms was not identified as a culprit in the 2006 spinach contamination event, the depth of the scare's economic effect upon growers and marketers is evident in this clamshell plastic container, carefully labeled "Organic," "Washed & Ready to Use" and, tellingly, "Contains No Spinach." With food fear spreading like a viral internet video, an entire year's worth of spinach was considered suspect and much of that was plowed under or otherwise destroyed. The costs of lost sales were sizable. In 2015, California growers—mainly in the Salinas and Imperial val-leys—produced spinach worth more than $190 million, a number sizably more than the $40 million from 2006.

Recently-Installed Fencing to Protect Crops from Pigs along
Cienega Road, Paicines

Paicines, in San Benito County, was the epicenter of a 2006 *E. coli* O157:H8 outbreak from an organic grower that ultimately was believed to contribute to 141 hospitalizations and three deaths, across 21 states. The USDA and FDA took nearly a year to isolate the geographical point of origin, and the exact cause remains speculative: blamed are wild swine breaking through fences that are assumed to have contaminated water supplies subsequently tapped for irrigation—or so the diagnosis went. The response from nearby growers was this formidable fencing, created to exclude wild pigs or other rooting animals from fields. Enough barbed wire and implied lethality shifts the scene from Virgilian agricultural idyll to an uncomfortable evocation of a prison yard.

Contains No Spinach, Earthbound Farm Organic Mix, 2006, Peter Goin.

Recently-Installed Fencing to Protect Crops from Pigs along Cienega Road, Paicines, 2010, Peter Goin.

BANC DIG 2017.14:Ag0126

Sign Advertising Live Oak Ranch Homes, Eastern Contra Costa County, 2006, Peter Goin.

Large House under Construction at Former Pear Orchard Site, near Locke and Snodgrass Slough, 2006, Peter Goin.

BANC DIG 2017.14:Ag00278

Winter View of Shredded Pepper Field Coverings, 2007, Peter Goin.

BANC DIG 2017.14:Ag01212

Sign Advertising Live Oak Ranch Homes, Eastern Contra Costa County

Brentwood, Oakley, and Byron in eastern Contra Costa County hold an area of some 12,000 acres remaining in farmland, according to the Brentwood Agricultural Land Trust, largely given over to U-pick operations and intensive urban-fringe farms that raise fresh-market sweet corn, tomatoes, and other produce. After World War II, the San Francisco Bay Area still had a substantial produce farming community; today, livestock ranching is the dominant use on lands zoned for agriculture, and much in decline. This sign advertises the build-outs at Live Oak Ranch, a subdivision in Oakley, that places packed-together homes on what was once prime farmland.

Large House under Construction at Former Pear Orchard Site, near Locke and Snodgrass Slough

Orchards are unwatered; the trees dead and in most cases wrested from the ground and set aside in shabby piles. The house—a mini-mansion of a sort—appears past Locke, west of Snodgrass Slough, where the Delta edges toward Sloughhouse and into Sacramento County. Exurban housing is a longstanding competitor of agriculture, and in this case, gained an upper hand. While crops, and especially tree crops, can provide a year-in, year-out income, overstated housing is subject to a particularly roller-coaster market, with a marked collapse in urban-fringe California from 2008–2011.

Wind Farm, Highway 111, Riverside County, 2007, Peter Goin.

BANC DIG 2017.14:Ag00618

Wind Farm, Highway 111, Riverside County

Not all farming in California is purely agricultural—blades turn on a wind farm near Palm Springs, California. In more verdant climates, such as Altamont Pass in eastern Alameda County, cattle and sheep may graze underneath the turbines. Forty years ago, the notion of "farming" energy might have seemed laughable. But given today's profusion of 10% ethanol signs on gasoline pumps, the production of energy from agriculture has new resonance—biogas, cogeneration, and ethanol from switchgrass or farm byproducts. While the gleaning of electricity from wind was practiced atop San Francisco apartments in the early 1900s, it took until the late 1970s for commercial wind energy to graduate to large-acreage ventures that collectively generated a sizable megawattage of grid-ready power. Wind turbines add a prickly upright contour, their tall towers contrasting with the prevalent rangeland shades of green or brown. Generally, wind farms are sited between cooler coastal areas and hot inland valleys, where marked temperature and pressure gradients produce sizable and persistent winds, as here near Palm Springs in Riverside County. And wind farms are often in prime raptor habitat, so birds lost to spinning rotors generate plenty of controversy. The debate puts the appropriateness of energy developments—with good or bad or indifferent ancillary environmental effects—in the same camp as discussions of agriculture. Talk of visual blight and environmental disruption has turned accusingly toward dispersed energy-providing technologies—farms of solar panels, wind farms, solar furnaces, geothermal wells, and even off-shore wind turbines.

Winter View of Shredded Pepper Field Coverings

Statues and road signs, relict buildings and field-side machinery, power grids and greenhouses are contributors to the function of California agriculture. What may seem to the uninitiated observer a cabinet of curiosities is utterly practical, making good sense to someone who recognizes the method and meaning of features on the land. Finding significance in those forms demands knowledge—in the words of cultural geographer Peirce Lewis, "the more you know, the more you see." Peppers can require protection from sunburn and the elements, and they bring good prices. With time and weathering, however, their shelters become shrouds.

Frost-Damaged Avocado Tree, Pauma Valley,
San Diego County, 2007, Peter Goin.

BANC DIG 2017.14:Ag00725

Frost-Damaged Avocado Tree, Pauma Valley, San Diego County

After a difficult 2006–2007 winter in which temperatures dropped low enough to savage the remnant citrus acreage in Southern California, there turned out to be sizable ancillary damage to commercial avocado trees that froze in San Diego County and elsewhere across the Southland. Massive chainsaw pruning followed, as here in Pauma Valley, with attempts made to keep trees alive that included the whitewashing of bark to prevent sunburn, retain water, repel borers and other pests, and stave off decay. Agriculture, even of durable tree crops, is not a set-it and forget it activity. It's a profession, and growers care deeply about their acreage and the crops planted on them, just as ranchers worry about the health of their livestock, and they will go the extra mile to save what's ailing.

Close-up of Walnut and Leaves, Sprayed to Prevent Sunburn, Tehama County

If freezes are a forever-risk to tree crops, especially those that flower early and require a bevy of pollinators, there are perils associated with good weather, too. Walnuts, and those at the edge of a sizable grove, do fine with incident light. But with the barrage of direct summer sun, walnuts can lose leaves and tree health to sunburn, which can add black sunburn spots to the walnuts themselves. A solution is reasonable enough: To keep those trees in full sun thriving, spray them with a white organic spray that increases reflection and minimizes sun damage. Predictably, there are various commercial sprays available that keep the trees from harm. Still, from the road, the effect is curious—until you understand what you're seeing.

Close-up of Walnut and Leaves, Sprayed to Prevent Sunburn, Tehama County, 2007, Peter Goin.

BANC DIG 2017.14:Ag00977

Bird House

Nesting boxes are just one of the social-ecological services that growers will provide between the rows of a grove. Whether a residence of convenience for migratory species or local songbirds, they offer a welcoming shelter for airborne travelers from afar (or near), and reflect the state of overall environmental health. Great fields of fruit and nut trees, so carefully maintained with fastidious watering and a carefully cleared understory, can seem bereft of life. Birds, attracted to the well-maintained houses, provide relief from starkness.

Bird House, Madera County, 2010, Peter Goin.

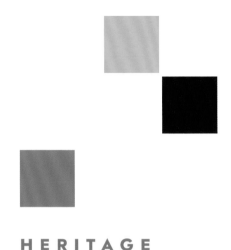

HERITAGE

IN CALIFORNIA AGRICULTURE "BIGNESS" IS SOMETHING RECOGNIZABLE AND SO HAS IT ALWAYS BEEN. Agriculture at an extensive scale began with Spanish—Mexican times in the 1770s. The scope of ranching and crop-growing enterprises—ever an expression of sheer ambition—were large, with land grants that put acreage for ranches or other agriculture in the hands of a few favored recipients, including early non-Hispanic arrivals. The story was tied to ambitions of the rancheros and *patrons*. They developed holdings in land and the cattle (sheep less often) that roamed the countryside, dodging grizzly bear, wolves, and rustlers. After missions were secularized under Mexican control, outsiders arrived with landholding ambitions of their own. Those included Charles M. Weber, a founder of what is now Stockton, California, who in 1845 received El Rancho

del Campo de los Franceses, a land grant of eleven square Spanish leagues that gave him control of some 48,000 acres. Charles Weber's neighbor to the north was the Swiss-born John (Johann) Sutter, whose New Helvetia, likewise eleven square leagues, included much of today's city of Sacramento. Each became a Mexican citizen to gain title to the land. The properties were prodigious in size, roamed by wildlife (elk, grizzly, geese, marine mammals, ducks, turtles, all overflown by the California condor) and used for ranching. Many were later subdivided, with ownership subject after statehood to legal challenge before the Board of California Land Commissioners. Such sprawling parcels were nearly impossible to control and maintain. Weber fared better than Sutter, who died impoverished, his holdings picked to pieces by squatters and court disputes. But in scale, the die was cast for the dimensions of agricultural parcels in California.

Livestock ranching was California's first sizable agricultural economy, along with growing crops to feed Native American acolytes, soldiers, clerics, and the Catholic missions and their slowly growing adjoining towns. With the Gold Rush and statehood came an era of agricultural invention and cropland agriculture spread far afield, from El Camino Real, especially into the Central Valley. Agriculture grew more important, and acquiring land was a recurring theme—the limitations were water supply and means to a market, which also generally meant by water, since there were no railroads until the 1860s.

Smallish irrigation-based communities were attempted in the late nineteenth century, notably in Southern California and locations along foothills of the Sierra Nevada in the San Joaquin Valley, where it was thought a Jeffersonian ideal of the yeoman farmer might flourish. That gave way to industrial agriculture, or as known now, agribusiness. Examples abound. Southern California's Tejon Ranch (est. 1843)

with a listing on the New York Stock Exchange (NYSE:TRC) at 270,000 acres, is the largest contiguous private property in California, with 90% of that area in conservation easements created in 2008. Grazing cattle, oil and gas, gravel and aggregate, almonds, pistachios, and wine grapes provide most of the Tejon Ranch income. The ranching and farming colossus Miller & Lux owned 1.5 million acres in California and the West, and controlled far more. A Bonanza Wheat era was initiated by Dr. Hugh Glenn, who owned 66,000 acres of land outright near Colusa. On it he raised a million bushels of wheat, which was coveted (and exported) worldwide, and for a time shipped 14,000 miles to Britain and elsewhere in Europe. From 1859—1929, the real value of California's crop output grew more than 25 times. There were profits aplenty to be earned from other forms of agriculture. By the late 1930s, the cotton-growing J.G. Boswell Company, based in Corcoran, gained its founder the title of "King of California," the name of a 2003 biography coauthored by Mark Arax. And in 2018 Arax published "A Kingdom from Dust" in *California Sunday Magazine* about the Resnicks, residents of Beverly Hills, California, who are the "biggest irrigated farmers in the world," owning 180,000 California acres. While Lynda is active in farmworker health and environmental justice issues, Stewart—age 81—is "the farmer who moved the rain," creating an empire of 121,000 irrigated acres, watering fifteen million almond, pistachio, and pomegranate trees. That says something about the scale of success in California farming.

Tulare, Kern, and Fresno counties regularly vie for the title of biggest agriculture income earner in the United States. Their agriculture is varied. By 1900, vegetable and fruit production was swelling, and technological innovation assured that another "heritage" of California, beyond skyward diversity and income, would be a human legacy of knowledge, mechanization, and ingenuity. It's worth remembering that today California's biggest landowners are corporations, many family-owned, involved in ranching, oil and natural gas production, timberland and forestry. Boom and bust cycles operate as conspicuously in the agricultural world as they do in mining, wildlife populations, popular fashions, or viral media. Partnerships grow strained and dissolve; legal challenges invalidate uses of land and water or upend short-lived monopolies. Foodstuffs or fashion items with a fanatical following such as ostrich feathers or turtle soup or hides and tallow or kiwifruit or acai berries turn out not to be quite as enduringly popular as their speculator-producers might hope. And in the end, there are more intricate stories where small, clever, ambitious, and often non-White farmers make California agriculture a venture with a heritage of ingenuity and experimentation. ■

Welcome to Salinas, Salad Bowl of the World, 2007, Peter Goin.

BANC DIG 2017.14:Ag00587

Welcome to Salinas, Salad Bowl of the World

If the portrait of Rancho Los Meganos was commissioned as a tribute to one person's accumulated conspicuous wealth, the claims broadcast on this sign near the Salinas city limits along Highway 101 are in the same spirit: a tribute to self—yet with a bit of truth-telling. Likely more lettuce, of many and varied types (from arugula and escarole to mizuna and romaine), ships from the Salinas Valley than any other single region in the world. And enticingly, the sign points straight at a large strawberry field adjoining the stretch of road. Between them, those two crops are big contributors to the Califorwnia agricultural economy, numbers 5 and 6 in value "out the farm gate" in 2015, with each bringing in well over $4 billion.

Rancho Los Meganos [Contra Costa County, California]

What is now eastern Contra Costa County once was the domain of Miwok and Yokut Native Americans. In Spanish the meaning of "Los Meganos" is, literally, "the dunes," and in 1835 Rancho Los Meganos was awarded by Alta California Governor José Castro to José Noriega, whose extensive properties included multiple square Spanish leagues of land in the South Bay. Each *legua geográfica*, a traditional unit of area, was a little less than 4,500 acres. The Los Meganos Mexican grant totaled roughly 13,000 acres, and was as dramatic in prospect as this panoramic painting, with ranchland stretching from present-day Clayton and Antioch to the San Joaquin River. After just two years Noriega sold the territory to John Marsh, a medical practitioner of a sort, despite his never earning a medical degree. Marsh accumulated a sizable cattle herd,

according to some observers, by billing a cow for any medical service rendered. All was not easy gain: his ranch was at the northern end of La Vereda del Monte, a path that ran north–south through several hundred miles of the Coast Ranges. That hardscrabble trail provided *mesteñeros*—thieves supposedly including Joaquin Murrieta—an escape route with stolen horses and cattle. Unsurprisingly, the grant would become contested territory, although eventually Marsh and his family would find their claim approved by federal authorities. Promising a beneficent climate and available land, Marsh heavily advertised his location and property

so it became the end-point of the California Trail and a kind of gateway to the larger San Francisco Bay area. On it he built a 7,000 square foot house from locally quarried stone, designed by San Francisco architect Thomas Boyd. In 1856 Marsh was murdered by three of his vaqueros, and his son and daughter inherited the mansion. With time, the children lost the property and it would come into the ownership of James T. Sanford of New York in 1871. This framed landscape portrait quite ably captures the site's splendor, the sizable stone Marsh house in the background, with riders on horseback nearing outlying corrals.

Rancho Los Meganos [Contra Costa County, California], ca. 1865,
Edward Jump [French painter, 1832–1883], Robert B. Honeyman Jr.
Collection of Early Californian and Western American Pictorial Material.
BANC PIC 1963.002:1329—FR

RANCHO LOS MEGANOS

Property of James T. Sanford of New York

The Chinese Vegetable Vendor

For all the big producers, much can be said about farming and selling small. Food consumers—and eating is something we all do—want to know who grows and sells our food. Seeing who is selling what is an act of communion, meeting our marketers, and the trend is not just a new one. "The Chinese Vegetable Vendor," reads a careful caption, scripted in a copperplate hand with fountain-pen ink. The undated photograph speaks to several themes: available fresh produce that can be purchased street-side, a vendor and a client whose straw-woven hats—in distinct styles—advertise wise protection from the prevailing sun, and a diversity of crops available: celery, grapes, squash of several types, eggplant, and assorted fruit. Such was the story of nineteenth-century California crops and daily life.

Chou Toua Chang and Daughter, Christina Chang at Fruit and Vegetable Stand, Northwest of Merced

The varieties of marketing strategies for California produce are considerably more inventive than what's proffered by the major chain groceries. A favorite for travelers who eschew the doubtful charms of the Interstate highway—where no one should focus on anything but traffic ahead—are roadside stands such as this one, on the western edge of Merced. A father—daughter team sell strawberries, with long rows of the plants alongside the modest stand. She was the voluble partner, but the fruit speaks for itself.

The Chinese Vegetable Vendor. Gelatin silver print. Scenes from Various San Francisco Bay Locations.

BANC PIC 1979.034:02—ALB

Chou Toua Chang and Daughter, Christina Chang at Fruit and Vegetable Stand, Northwest of Merced, 2007, Peter Goin.

Stockdale Ranch, Haying Scene

A remarkable Carleton Watkins photograph captures Chinese laborers and a few non-Chinese bringing in a hay harvest. The entwined technology is as notable as the lofty haystack, with lines and pulleys and cables and horses hauling the hay to considerable heights. Those stacks cured in place and would be fed to large herds of sheep and cattle assembling then in the southern San Joaquin Valley in the 1880s. Kern County went unchartered as a county until 1866; local agricultural colonies were established scattershot in the 1880s, about the time that this view is provisionally dated. Agriculture, and in particular, the impounding and diversion of water for irrigation, started to become a complicated issue in the mid-1860s, when intimations appeared of an epic California contest: How can water be used? The question of whether diversion of water was acceptable under either riparian or appropriative water rights reached the California Supreme Court (more than once) in the 1880s, to be resolved in a case that pitted Henry Miller and Charles Lux against James Ben-Ali Haggin, who owned land upriver in the Sierra Nevada foothills. Although lawsuits began in 1879, they were only settled by the California Supreme Court in 1886, with a 4–3 decision (*Lux v. Haggin*, 69 Cal. 255, 10 P. 674). Opulent hay fields and much-engaged laborers are, therefore, only a part of the story. The rest, as is so often the case in California agriculture, was resolved by law books and Solomonic legal decisions; hardly the stuff of a dramatic view, at least for the non-lawyering public.

Stockdale Ranch, Haying Scene, ca. 1887, Carleton E. Watkins.
Albumen print. Kern County Views from the Keith-McHenry-Pond family.

BANC PIC 1952.002:1—AX

George Shima, the Potato King, Plowing... on Lands near Stockton
The arrivals came from around the world: Chinese, English, Filipino, German, Hawaiian, Hmong, Irish, Indian/South Asian, Italian, Japanese, Lao, Mexican, Pacific Islander, Russian, Salvadorian, Samoans, Spanish, Swiss—and, of course, African American, Latina(o), and other Hispanic. They sought a stake—or just employment—in California agriculture only to find ownership or labor options not always easily obtained. Asian American immigrants were especially hard-treated, plagued with anti-foreigner laws passed down by the U.S. Congress or the California legislature. Success could still arrive: George Shima (1864–1926) was a Japanese immigrant known as the Potato King, here seen plowing one of his fields, elegantly attired in necktie and vest, in the Delta near Stockton.

George Shima, the Potato King, Plowing..., ca. 1915. Ira B. Cross, collector. Gelatin silver print. Photographs of Agricultural Laborers in California collected in connection with his book, *A History of the Labor Movement in California, Berkeley, Calif.*, University of California Press, 1935.

BANC PIC 1905.02724—PIC

While it was Chinese immigrants who were targeted first for discrimination in landholding and labor opportunities, many a Japanese farmer was singled out in years leading up to World War II. Japanese farmers were phenomenally successful in the produce and floral industries into the early 1940s, controlling more than 200,000 acres of land on 6,000 farms—many of those stellar fruit tree and truck farming operations in the Santa Clara Valley. For a time, nearly a hundred percent of tomatoes, strawberries, and divers peppers were Japanese-raised, and farms were passed through the generations: issei (Japanese born, first generation), nisei (American-born, second generation), and sansei (third generation). Japanese American-owned agricultural operations often provided nursery and greenhouse crops for San Francisco Bay Area residents, which produced cut flowers and live plants that would flow outward from the East Bay where they were grown along the interurban Key Route in communities such as Richmond and El Cerrito. As population grew, the nurseries came paradoxically to be seen as unwanted, and home sites were considered more useful than greenhouses. Once plentiful, many Japanese American nurseries have now closed, but left behind is a legacy that literally grows in many a yard or other favored location. The heritage is not solely in agricultural bounty; it is in art, living memory, and writing. David Mas Masumoto and his daughter Nikiko raise peaches, nectarines, and raisins south of Fresno, and his writing, which includes *Epitaph for a Peach, Four Seasons in Five Senses*, and seven other books, chronicle experiences of a Japanese American farmer in the San Joaquin Valley. A welter of Alien Land Laws were part and parcel of California land and labor life from the late nineteenth century onward. The federal Chinese Exclusion Act of 1882 was but a beginning, and laws discriminating against foreign, and in particular East Asian, ownership of land in California were applied

with considerable force. The FSA is best remembered today for its "Historical Section" archives, under the direction of Roy Stryker, which collected more than 170,000 memorable images from dozens of photographers including Arthur Rothstein, Walker Evans, Dorothea Lange, Ben Shahn, and Gordon Parks. But during World War II, a separate section of the FSA was charged, along with the War Relocation Authority, with selling confiscated Japanese landholdings, under the terms of Executive Order 9066, which forcibly moved citizens of Japanese ancestry to locations including the Heart Mountains of Wyoming; Tule Lake, California, and, of course, Manzanar, near Lone Pine, California, east of the Sierra Nevada. Some 120,000 were interned; two-thirds were natural born citizens of the U.S.; many lost their land. In 1988, the U.S. Congress acknowledged that these events were "motivated largely by racial prejudice, wartime hysteria, and a failure of political leadership."

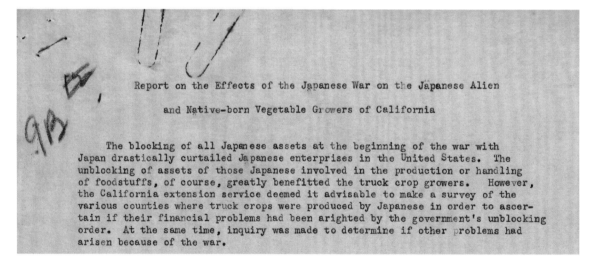

Report on the Effects of the Japanese War on the Japanese Alien and Native-Born Vegetable Growers of California, December 29, 1941. [Excerpt from letter] W.R. Ralston Papers Relating to California Agriculture.

BANC MSS 99/195 carton 2:1

Japanese Information Bureau

The marquee atop a stout brick façade announces the Japanese Information Bureau, a venture of Frank N. Aikawa and Ben K. Kaneka. While the photograph's date is uncertain, the venture was certainly a going concern in the 1920s or '30s, and long before World War II, since this appeared in a 1935 monograph by Berkeley economics professor Ira Cross. The "Bureau" is a reminder of the presence and influence of Japanese American businesses, its sign advertising "General Contractors," "Interpreters," "Real Estate," and "Farm Hands." The early decades of the twentieth century were not easy times for non-Caucasian (or Hispanic) entrepreneurs or laborers in California. Asians fared worst. There were budding tensions, with rising xenophobia and nativism in the early 1900s, especially after Japan's success in expanding its empire during the Russo–Japanese War. Those concerns were somewhat distant ones, overall, for California farmers—whether Japanese American or otherwise. Almost as worthy of mention as the photograph is its collector, Ira B. Cross (1880–1977). A descendent of New England pilgrims, Cross earned a bachelor's and master's degree at the University of Wisconsin, and after joining the Socialist Party in 1906 he would complete a PhD at Stanford University in 1909. Cross taught there until moving to Berkeley in 1914, where he was a professor of labor economics until retirement in 1951. His *History of the Labor Movement in California* is an acknowledged classic, and his papers are today still an ongoing trove of information for researchers at The Bancroft Library.

Japanese Information Bureau, Ira B. Cross, collector. Gelatin silver print. Photographs of Agricultural Laborers in California collected in connection with his book, *A History of the Labor Movement in California*, Berkeley, University of California Press, 1935.

R. Waltz and G.D. Greenan Harvesting Cork

Cork is a remarkable crop and grown to one degree or another in all countries that border the Mediterranean Sea, most conspicuously in Spain and Portugal, which today produce nearly two-thirds of the world's cork supply. Woodbridge Metcalf (1888–1972), a forestry professor and extension specialist at the University of California, in 1914 began a 58-year association supporting studies of forestry at Berkeley. Among his interests—and concerns—was cork, used not only in bottles as a stopper, but with widespread strategic uses: as sound (acoustical) insulation in battleships, where it covered flooring and padded walls, and in many an industrial application. During both World Wars, Metcalf worked on cork production in California, examining plantings in sites as diverse as the Napa State Hospital, southern Sonoma, Oroville, Mendocino, Monrovia, and Chico, California, where earlier horticulturalists and foresters had introduced cork oaks (*Quercus suber*). He attempted a suite of experimental plantings, since there was concern that military and political uncertainty in Mediterranean cork-growing regions might choke off supply. The crucial weakness in California's cork production proved in part climatic differences, but more, an absence of skilled cork-strippers, still today a highly specialized vocation in the southwestern Iberian Peninsula. Harvest should never hurt the tree, and after a low-quality first extraction at twenty-plus years, can be repeated every 8–14 years. Now-monumental cork oaks planted in 1925, after UC Davis was established on what used to be the UC Berkeley Experimental Farm, have never had their cork stripped. A description by Metcalf of the harvesting process merits repetition: "On the larger trees it is advisable to make two vertical cuts to remove the cork. Wooden wedges and a method of tapping them with mallet are shown. The cork was removed from this tree in two sections with very little damage to the cambium. Some vertical cracks appear in the inner bark layer after a few hours." Imported cork today goes into shoe welts, spaceship heat shields, laser printer paper-pickups, and as a slab or frog for orchid arrangements. Oh, and there is that traditional use, dating back to Classical times, as a wine stopper—for wine makers who decline to use Stelvin screw caps.

R. Waltz and G.D. Greenan Harvesting Cork, 1940, Woodbridge Metcalf, FM002910a_ii, Accession 2701b, Courtesy of the Marian Koshland Bioscience and Natural Resources Library, University of California, Berkeley.

Hop Fields on Sacramento River Bottom Land, Finest in the World
Through the first half of the twentieth century, hops were an
important California crop, whose fortune and producers
were likely affected by Prohibition (1920–1933). The long
vines, extending up to eighteen feet tall, were never easily
harvested, and labor conditions through the mid-twentieth-
century were opprobrious. Labor actions followed. The
role of hop (or hops; the semantic debates over syntax are
lurid) in California are scattershot but profound. Hopland,
California, in Mendocino County, keeps its name even
though the hops are long gone—by and large moved to
Oregon and the Yakima Valley of Washington. Among the
more spectacular labor conflicts in California was a hop
riot among workers in 1913, at the 642-acre Durst Ranch in
Wheatland (Yuba County), which resulted in four deaths and
a multitude of injuries. Durst, a local hops grower, promised
jobs to any harvester who showed up; 2,800 did, far more
than could be housed, and the conditions were deplorable.
Local authorities blamed the Industrial Workers of the World
(IWW), in what proved the first major labor confrontation
in twentieth-century California. Wet hops used in the
booming West Coast craft brewing industry are returning
to California, though in far less quantity now than in the
1940s and 1950s.

Hop Fields on Sacramento River Bottom Land, Finest in the World, 1910–1915, McCurry Foto Company, San Francisco.
Gelatin silver print. From album Rivergarden Farms.

BANC PIC 1977.019:14—ALB

Berkeley Fruit Supply Co.

This bustling Berkeley business, at 2088–2086 University Avenue, is mentioned in a 1916 Polk-Husted Berkeley City Directory, but this view could be from a decade or two later. The scene speaks to prosperity, and significantly, in front of the store are two overall-clad workers and a third person (perhaps the owner?) in a straw boater and a dapper suit, all three Asian. Berkeley after the turn of the century was a growing and changing place. No less diverse are the fruits and vegetables: long clusters of bananas dangling from the stem, squash, chestnuts, Brussels sprouts, heads of lettuce, and garlands of onions.

Berkeley Fruit Supply Co., undated photograph, Alfred Greene and Max W. Greene.

Gelatin silver print. Berkeley and Oakland Business Scenes.

BANC PIC 1988.063.03—PIC

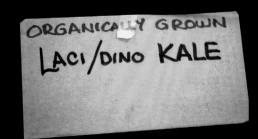

Labels, Monterey Market, Berkeley, 2007, Peter Goin.

Labels, Monterey Market, Berkeley

Amaranth, dandelion, Chioggia beets, parsley root, cilantro, Brussels sprouts, Pixie tangerines, Laci/Dino kale, green/red kohlrabi, Nakamura royal apricots, bok choy, and romaine hearts reveal through signs the diversity of California agriculture. In 1961, Tom Takumi Fujimoto (1905–1993) and Mary Nobori Fujimoto (1909–1987) founded Monterey Market in Berkeley. When Tom was 15, he emigrated to the United States, arriving first in the Pacific Northwest. His travels continued next to Los Angeles where with his wife Mary, he became a celery farmer in the Dominguez Hills area. Two months after the Japanese bombing of Pearl Harbor (1941), U.S. President Franklin D. Roosevelt signed Executive Order 9066 ordering all Japanese Americans to evacuate the West Coast. This resulted in the relocation of approximately 120,000 people, many of whom were American citizens, to one of ten internment camps located across the country. Tom and Mary lost their farm and home as they and their three children were first interned at Gila, Arizona, and then transferred to the camp at Topaz, Utah. After the war, Tom worked as a tenant farmer in Homedale, Idaho, but in 1948, the Fujimoto family resettled in the Bay Area, where Tom worked in stores owned by Mary's brothers. In 1954, Tom and Mary opened their own Acme Market in Oakland where they catered to the multicultural neighborhood clientele. Given the success of their produce store, Tom and Mary decided in 1980 to expand their business and purchased the former Louis Store at 1550 Hopkins Street in Berkeley. The Monterey Market is at the same location to this day, providing produce, groceries, dairy, wine, beer, and other locally grown items to its customers. Although Tom and Mary are now deceased, Bill and Ken Fujimoto continue to run the family business in the spirit and memory of their parents.

Fourth Annual Picnic Basket Programme

The Berkeley campus is located where it is today, historian William Rorabaugh writes, in part because the foggy summer climate and the swift climb of the sizable East Bay Hills meant the site chosen at Founder's Rock was patently "undesirable" for agriculture. Those who live today in Berkeley, where summer fog careens through the Golden Gate and slaps against the campus, would agree. In practice that meant a considerable part of applied crop, rangeland, technical, and irrigation research had to take place where it was better suited. Experience and climate studies found the best venue for an agricultural testing site—the University Farm—would draw on fertile soils in lower Putah Creek near what is now modern-day Davis: "The legislature of 1905 made an appropriation to purchase a farm for the College of Agriculture of the University of California and appointed a commission to select a site. The farm of 780 acres was chosen in the summer of 1907 [part of the award winning Jerome B. Davis stock farm], and during the following year construction was begun upon on the first buildings … instruction to regular students began in January, 1909." Establishment of the University Farm was celebrated in a 1908 picnic. A campus emphasis at first limited to matters agricultural blossomed in 1959, when Regents designated UC Davis and UC Riverside as "general campuses," expanding the curricular scope to liberal arts and sciences, sizably increasing student numbers. After 150 years, the University of California system now includes experimental farms, research stations, and—since 1965—750,000 acres set aside on 39 public, NGO, and private natural reserve sites dappled around the state. And on the 21st of April, 2018, the Annual UC Davis Picnic was held, a still-cherished event after 104 years.

Fourth Annual Picnic Basket Programme, May 11, 1912. Records of the College of Agriculture, University of California Archives, BANC CU-20, box 22:8

Michael Gale and Angus Bull, Chileno Valley Ranch, Marin County, 2006, Peter Goin.

BANC DIG 2017.14:Ag0230

Michael Gale and Angus Bull... Refrigerator Full of Eggs ...
Fulton Valley Natural Chicken ... Orchard Rules for U-pick ...
Agriculture without marketing is essentially a hobby, and small farmers who want to sell what they make will advertise with pride of product. In an age of abundant skepticism about food safety and quality and the origins of food, the saying "know your farmer" approaches the status of a mantra. Getting to know where food comes from as an alternative can involve a household's members in picking, procuring, and otherwise acquiring and processing— "putting up"—food. Four views suggest the range of possibilities. At Chileno Valley Ranch in West Marin County, Mike and Sally Gale run an Angus beef operation, where purchasers can pre-purchase a share of a cow or steer (whole, half, quarter) that will in time be butchered, cut, wrapped, and picked up by subscribers from a certified meat cutter. Realizing there would be gaps in the production year, the Gales later planted a highly varied orchard of heirloom dwarf apples trees, which ranch visitors can pick when in season, entering the fenced-off orchard with a five-gallon bucket, and paying by the pound. Fulton Valley chicken is raised with comparable care, as the sign explains, and is widely available around the San Francisco Bay Area. At the Wolfe Ranch, in eastern Contra Costa County, the late-spring cherry season (Bing, White Rainier, Van) brings U-pick aficionados from all over who will "buy what they pick." That such rules have to be spelled out is a reflection of the urban—rural divide, but good and stern advice. Finally, in likely thousands of locations around California, small signs advertise "fresh farm eggs," and a turn up a modest road, paved or not, brings buyers to a refrigerator where eggs can be purchased, often with payment left in a basket or jar. This is not the stuff of industrial farming dreams, but it certainly permits purchasers across several generations to find a connection to their food.

Refrigerator Full of Eggs, McCormack Ranch, Rio Vista, 2007, Peter Goin.

Kern County, ca. 1887, Carleton Watkins. Albumen print. Keith-McHenry-Pond family pictorial collection.

BANC PIC 1952.002:19

Kern County

Signs of a certain kind of domestic agricultural tranquility are evident—a heritage unto itself. In the United States, the family farm is a source of nostalgia, even in California where such ventures are often secured as LLCs or otherwise corporatized. The vision Watkins acquired (and from what vantage point?) is of work and prosperity, akin to ornamental (and paid-for) vignettes that once surrounded the borders of bird's-eye views or maps of the day. Four farmers stand in a Kern County barnyard. One holds the bridle of a stud horse; a second has the collar of what appears to be a greyhound; the third feeds quite the poultry collection: geese, chickens, turkeys, a duck or two, and what appear to be a couple of guinea fowl. A handsomely appointed barn is at one side; an oak on the other side of the yard, with more stands of oak in the distance. The Watkins portrait documents success and a pastoral scene.

Fulton Valley Natural Chicken (sign), Magnani Poultry,
Berkeley. 2007, Peter Goin.

Toting Chickens in Wooden Cage, 1890—1893, Norman H. Reed.
N.H. Reed Photograph Album of Santa Barbara and Vicinity.

Toting Chickens in Wooden Cage

Some arrivals came for California land, for others that was the stuff of dreams: they hoped for work and an income, even if spare. Chickens packed into a hand-built cage speak of austerity, with the cargo carrier's clothing all but in shreds. For these chickens there is little doubt about their stew pot destination, and travel conditions were various steps down from the posh. Perhaps curiously (unless you happen to be a chicken fancier), chickens are back in fashion for the self-reliant backyard farmer. National Book Award and Pulitzer Prize-winning author Alice Walker in 2011 published The *Chicken Chronicles*, a reflection on cherished time spent with bird-companions at her Mendocino, California, home. The book's subtitle(s) pay tribute to her charges: *Sitting with the Angels Who Have Returned with My Memories: Glorious, Rufus, Gertrude Stein, Splendor, Hortensia, Agnes of God, the Gladyses, & Babe: A Memoir*. A 2018 *Washington Post* article discussed the new Silicon Valley cult of chicken-raisers charting egg production, ritually wheeling high-end chicken tractors (or arks) across lawns, and bringing host gifts of carefully curated multi-hued eggs. A world apart from this view.

Greenhouse Row, Chac-Chuo Farm, Oasis, Riverside County, 2007, Peter Goin.

BANC DIG 2017.14:Ag00651

Interior of Greenhouse, Showing Water Spinach, Chac-Chuo Farm, Oasis,
Riverside County, 2007, Peter Goin.

Greenhouse Row, Chac-Chuo Farm ... Interior of Greenhouse

The American diet, and certainly that of Californians, is vastly broadened by a multicultural population, and a long esplanade of greenhouses make possible raising a remarkable variety of crops, some of them for a big swath of the state's population, in other cases just for niche markets. A greenhouse doorway offers a portal into another universe, Wonderland-like. The careful framing of a particular view is an age-old motif in agriculture and art, repeated often in orange crate labels crafted by the Schmidt Lithograph Company of San Francisco, beginning in the 1880s. An inevitable sense of wizardry is invoked by pulling back a curtain and looking in, even when what lies inside is water spinach—one of a remarkably varied assortment of Asian greens grown to sate an increasing demand from ethnic and farmers markets, and a seasonal delicacy stocked by grocers and served up by Asian restaurants. Heritage, in other words, invokes not just heirloom crops and heritage animal breeds, it also draws in the very diversity of California's Native American past, its greatly varied sequence of immigrants, laborers, visitors, and admirers. A California made up of a monocultural population is almost as bizarre a thought as trying to imagine the state with just one or two crops. Diversity may be California's greatest heritage.

CLOSED Fruit Stand, Lodi California

And in the end, there is the fruit stand. They are vernacular ornaments, cobbled together, set up fieldside, hopefully with some spare safe space for cars and pickup trucks and bicycles or Über and Lyft ride-share passengers to stop, sniff, sample, and speed away with whatever good stuff is there for the purchasing. The stands stay there, part of the agricultural marketing firmament, even when there isn't produce to sell: out comes the "CLOSED" sign. The most modest stands are oft-times tended by family members; the bigger commercial stands will have more variety (and, truth be told, it is always a worry that on the largest stands, sourcing of produce may be less than local). Farmers markets are another means of connecting with the buying public, and any feature that brings good safe food is for the best.

***Orchard Rules for U-pick, Wolfe Ranch, Brentwood**, 2007, Peter Goin.*

CLOSED Fruit Stand, Lodi, 2008, Peter Goin.

BANC DIG 2017.14:01120

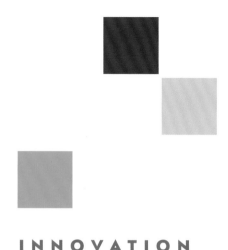

INNOVATION

THE INNOVATIONS THAT CALIFORNIA GROWERS AND TECHNOLOGY AND FINANCE AND EXPERIMENTERS PROVIDE AGRICULTURE ARE LEGION, AND MAYBE EVEN LEGENDARY. Diet here and abroad are the huge beneficiaries. Just how and why? It's a coat of many colors. Certainly, a part of the story is "equipment" and the contributors are familiar names. The Jacuzzi Brands Corporation, as the firm is now known, was formed in 1915. Originally the Jacuzzi family made propellers for boats and airplanes, switching later to manufacturing the crucial deep well pumps that draw up groundwater for irrigation. Back in the day, just a few city blocks from Jacuzzi's production facility on San Pablo Avenue was the Berkeley Pump Corporation, established in 1937. In terms of technical exploits there was always help available from the

UC Berkeley campus a few of miles up University Avenue. Water in California is the agricultural be-all and end-all—it doesn't happen without a water supply. In an era of climate change and drought that has irremediably altered California agriculture, water conservation can reduce costs, so tree crop growers adopt drip irrigation, with its added benefit of permitting the addition of carefully measured inputs of fertilizer, minerals, and other soil amendments directly into irrigation water. California crops require innovative farm equipment, tread-driven dozers, and specialty devices that can machine-harvest berries, or olives, or jalapeño peppers. Innovation may be the magic word for California agriculture.

The intellectual property involved is formidable. Plant breeding provided timely innovation. The elegant Santa Rosa botanist, agronomist, and plant-breeding scientist Luther Burbank (1849–1926) would develop 800 plant varieties, among them the Santa Rosa plum, nectarines, the Wickson plum, and the freestone peach. Grazing management in California picked up where the rather raw Spanish–Mexican *Two Years Before the Mast* hide-and-tallow era left off, embracing formal range science. Grazing models appropriate for the Great Plains were mothballed in the face of a drastically different summer-dry climate, and where relict ranches extended for tens of thousands of acres. By 2000, practices like creating conservation easements made it possible for ranchers, using livestock, to contribute to environmental improvement. Selective grazing could knock back exotic weeds, safeguard streams and water supply, protect endangered species and other wildlife, and embrace concepts like carbon sequestration and elongated wildlife corridors. When mechanical engineers at UC Davis in the 1970s assisted in the creation of equipment that could machine-pick tomatoes, campus geneticists and agronomists bred a tomato that withstood mechanized harvest. Since agricultural innovation requires capital, that required

production loans and amenable bankers, and there a great pioneer was A.P. Giannini. His Bank of Italy allowed middle-class citizens, immigrants included, to open accounts, and he created satellite offices—branch banks—that made possible agricultural loans for equipment, seed, and other yearly expenses. Banking, pump manufacturing, the development of specialized equipment for uses eventually adopted all over the world—all show how innovation is at the core of agricultural production.

Experimentation was, and is, a potent force in agriculture, whether engineered by small-farm breeders, by cooperative extension agents or industry agronomists, or by geneticists operating at the plant selection or genomic level. Innovation in agriculture, with corresponding changes at the farm or landscape scale, has brought a constant stream of novel crops, cultivars, and animal types into the state. Old breeds and races are introduced from Europe, Central Asia, West Africa, South Asia, China or Siberia. Routinely, plants or breeds recently developed in other parts of the Mediterranean realm are test-planted in California; the University of California's Agricultural Experiment Stations, like privately supported industry crop research boards, devote no small energy to finding tree- and field-crop strains or animals breeds that are better—or entirely original. Novel varieties may be engineered or discovered in the western hemisphere, as was the navel orange—a mutant blood sport found by American missionaries in Bahia, Brazil, in the 1810s, and introduced to California in 1870 as the "Bahia Navel." Many another important New World crop has come to California, including maize (corn, whether feeder or sweet), tomatoes, avocados, potatoes, assorted beans, and, of course, grains that have moved north such as quinoa or amaranth. The examples are too many to spell out in entirety.

Dairy Carousel Operation, Johann Dairy, Fresno County, 2006, Peter Goin.

BANC DIG, 2017.14:Ag00459

Dairy Carousel Operation, Johann Dairy, Fresno County
Turning and turning in a widening gyre... The cows jostle for access, enjoying their time on the slowly revolving carousel or "rotary milking parlor," where milking machines monitor production. Initially, the carousel was called the Rotolactor, developed by the Borden Company and put to work in 1930 in New Jersey. But New Zealand and Germany each provided improvements to the early milking carousel tech-nology, which has grown considerably since the 1990s. Each cow is identified by a transponder ear tag or an implanted RFID chip or both, so the amount of milk she contributes to big holding tanks is recorded, and each cow's milking session information goes into a database. The enormous milking carousels increasingly seen in California dairies move in a slow circle, offering each bovine passenger a gentle excursion while she is relieved of up to forty pounds of milk—twice a day, sometimes three-times daily. No sooner does one cow back off the carousel, thanks to a spritz of water to the face, than another walks on to start her ride. California-scale production dairies are a world apart from the small to medium dairies in Wisconsin or Vermont, where operations are smaller scale. The average Tulare County dairy had nearly 1,700 cows in 2015, while the typical Wisconsin dairy counted 146 cows. Capital intense—and the word intense is carefully chosen—the widespread adoption of the milking carousel is a peculiarly Californian combination, taking advantage of weather and climate (not so much moisture), technological expertise (the time-in-motion efficiencies developed for industry by Frederick Winslow Taylor), and awareness that a population of forty million resident demands cream and milk, half-and-half, butter, and cheese. Nor is a single carousel the paragon of size these days. Some dairies have two or even three carousels turning, running twenty-four hours a day with multiple shifts of workers and producing milk products sufficient for a small city. But small dairies persist and are major contributors to organic milk production.

Two Unidentified Workers Logging Data and Supervising Samples inside the Revolving Dairy Carousel
In the early days of Europeanized California, record keeping was a matter of ledgers and wooden file cab-inets, handwritten notes, and certificates of pedigree. Now it's different. When one or two thousand cows are going through two or three milking sessions a day, those paper records are nothing easily maintained. Instead, and perhaps thankfully, there are digitally signed nametags and computer chips that can be read for each cow as she sways into the stanchion or, better yet, into a slot on the milking carousel. Workers still need to monitor the milking operation, ensuring that all teats are milked, that each cow has sufficient time to let down her milk and, in turn, have that harvested. The human component is still essential—no longer involving hand-milking, but making sure the machines work as they should, leaving a cow relieved of a considerable burden. An average cow will produce about 21,000 pounds of milk per year; divide by eight (pounds per gallon) to get the total: more than 2,500 gallons per year. The record keeping helps detect rises and falls in production, which can suggest remedial action. A dairy cow's results are as closely monitored as the on-base percentage of a baseball professional, or the quarter-mile times of a training racehorse. The terminology is slightly bombastic: peak and summit milk production, records and summary values. A peak producer can provide eight to twelve gallons per day, and the purported record is held by a Wisconsin cow that produced 72,000 pounds of milk (more than 8,000 gallons) in a year. Suffice it to say, an 800-cow herd can each DAY produce a large tanker-truckload of milk. Little wonder the largest single contributor to farm-gate income in California is slotted under the entry of "milk and cream": $7.6 billion in 2013; $9.36 billion in 2014; $6.3 billion in 2015.

Two Unidentified Workers Logging Data and Supervising Samples inside the Revolving Dairy Carousel, 2006, Peter Goin.

Bull Lockhaven Alcartra Pietertje, Holstein-Friesian Association of America, Certificate of Registry. Otis H. Lockhart records, Los Angeles.

BANC MSS 2010/192 v.12

Bull Lockhaven Alcartra Pietertje

Improvement in activities such as dairying is more than a matter of producer size. Making sure of breeding and productivity of the cows is crucial to a dairy's success, so owners keep detailed records of each animal, including cow and bull, to find the best combination. Perhaps unsurprisingly, until the 1950s, dairies tended to be in relatively close proximity to cities, whether in the San Francisco Bay Area, in Sacramento, or in Southern California. The milk has to travel to its destination, and until truck travel delivery was fully developed, dairies would send someone to pick up milk cans, or the producers would deliver their milk to a central processing plant, where it would undergo the usual separation of cream from milk, homogenization, and pasteurization. The biggest producers now process their milk at a clean plant next to the milking facility, close by the cows. The Berkeley Farms Dairy began in 1908 in South Berkeley and continued purchasing milk from dairies in Alameda and Contra Costa counties until 1998, when Berkeley Farms was purchased by Dean Foods.

[Feeding Kid Goats]

Rampant cuteness and conventional small animal dairying offer a sense of how kid goats were handled. A mother's milk has value, so offspring are fed and form their own kid-goat society. While some female goats (or sheep or calves) are kept as replacement animals, males are steered toward being the center of attraction in a meal of *cabrito*, a festive food favored by more than a few groups (Hispanic, Sikh, Hindu, Muslim) in California. Dairying sports a remarkably long human history, producing not just milk for drinking and cheese-making (*chèvre*, an artisanal cheese, is a superior use for surplus liquid milk). In the early days of domestication, maybe 15,000 years ago, herders realized that milk—rife with fermentable sugars—could be turned into an intoxicating alcoholic beverage. In more than a few parts of the world today, milk from camels, yaks, sheep, goats, meet the same purpose. The charm of young animals, whatever the breed, keeps its allure.

[Feeding Kid Goats], Frank Adams. Lantern slide. California Agriculture Photographs.

BANC PIC 1959.085 LAN Box 10 (#164)

The Mammoth Blackberry
(Natural Size)
Cross between Texas Early and the common wild blackberry of California, raised from seed planted by J. H. Logan
of Santa Cruz, Cal. Ripens last of May.

The Mammoth Blackberry, 1880–1890, George Webb. Albumen print.

BANC PIC 1984.070

The Mammoth Blackberry

"Cross between Texas Early and the common wild blackberry of California, raised from seed planted by J.H. Logan of Santa Cruz, Cal. Ripens last of May," reads the caption text of this ebullient fruit. Monterey and Santa Cruz counties are major source areas for blackberries, raspberries, blueberries, and loganberries. Field workers harvest fruit to small baskets, move those swiftly to chillers, and once the sugars are stabilized by cooling, on to market. A certain boastful exuberance and even euphoria—"the mammoth blackberry"—is a frequent theme in Golden State farming, where more is better and bigger is best. Experiments, even in the nineteenth century, up-bred fruits and vegetables improving on earlier forms. Rudolph Boysen is credited with growing experiments that produced the Boysenberry, George Darrow and Walter Knott transplanted vines to Knott's farm in Buena Park. J. H. Logan of Santa Cruz was the original breeder of the still-extant "Loganberry." The tasty berries went into pies baked by Cordelia (Mrs.) Knott, and Knott's Berry Farm was on its way to fame. Success was a matter of building a better mousetrap, and it involved careful plant breeding—recalling to mind the long-ago peas of Brother Mendel.

Green Tomatoes

Tomatoes are an eccentric signature of local California life. Hothouse heirloom tomatoes appear in May and June (and in quantity, later), and canning tomatoes come on in force as fall arrives, harvested by great machines that in the 1970s replaced workers picking by hand. Most tomatoes for paste and sauce are cooked down and preserved, to be rehydrated when needed. These, however, are some of the "other" tomatoes: lurid green when picked. What's discarded in the field is anything blushing even remotely "ripe" or red. These green tomatoes are fast-chilled, stored at near-freezing temperatures, and then "ripened" by gassing that reddens the fruit, making it slicing-ready for use in fast-food outlets and in off-season months.

Green Tomatoes, 2006, Peter Goin.

BANC DIG 2017.14:Ag00151

LETTUCE CAPITAL OF
THE UNITED STATES ←—SALINAS—→ HOME OF THE GUAYULE
RUBBER INDUSTRY

Salinas Chamber of Commerce Statement on Guayule Rubber
Innovation may at times be as much a matter of timing
and necessity as raw conceptual brainpower. Conceived
of during World War II as a rubber substitute, "guayule"
(*Parthenium argentatum*) was introduced to the Salinas
Valley. A prevailing fear in the late 1930s and into the '40s
was that an increasingly militant Germany and especially
Japan would block access to natural rubber sources in
Southeast Asia and South America. Raising a new Salinas
Valley crop as part of the war effort was clearly conceived
to be a patriotic duty—and potentially a profitable crop to fill
in for rubber shortages. Guayule proved an underwhelming
financial success, and it turned out there were synthetic
rubber substitutes to be found: By 1964, synthetic rubber
made up 75 percent of the market, and a brief effort in
the Salinas Valley on behalf of rubber independence was
vanquished to mention in the archives. Especially noteworthy
is the text at the bottom of the page (part of the letterhead),
which shows fine ambition.

Salinas Chamber of Commerce Statement on Guayule Rubber,
March 14, 1942, Excerpt from Fred S. McCarger letter. W.R. Ralston
papers relating to California agriculture.

BANC MSS 99/195 carton 1:11

March 14th, 1942
The Truman Committee of the Senate
Washington, D. C.

Gentlemen:

Senator Sheridan Downey has asked me to
prepare for your use, a statement in regard
to guayule rubber.

Personally, I feel that the Government could not
have done better than they have done in placing
the production of guayule rubber in the hands
of the United States Forest Service and in the
selection of the personnel in that department. The
innumerable delays caused to the Forest Service
through Governmental red tape, are certainly
heart-rending under the circumstances when
every minute counts. It would seem that some of
these rules and regulations, which are geared to
peacetime, could be speeded up at this time. On
the other hand, the results that have been obtained
are phenomenal considering all the hindrances,

For 15 years we have been working to get
Government recognition of guayule rubber and we
have been blocked at every turn of the road. There
are some indications that those interests or some
others, are continuing to make it just as difficult as
possible to get the true information in regard to

guayule rubber before the American people. I hope
that your committee will see to it that all the true
information is gathered, that all possible theories
of planting, growing and milling are tried and that
every pound of seed possible is secured, so that we
can get as large a production of rubber as possible
in 1943 and 1944 in this country. Those in charge
of the project at Salinas must be given a greater
rein if we are going to get an all out production by
that time.

There is in existence, about 560 acres of mature
eleven year old shrubs and 100 acres of one to six
year old plants. These would produce probably
around 3,000 pounds of under-resinated rubber
per acre. as similar fields went 2,850 pounds per
acre in 1941, however, I presume these fields
should be kept for seed production for another
year or two. There are approximately 20 acres
of seedlings, which were planted late in the
summer here at Salinas, and a quarter of an acre
of seedlings at the California State Experimental
Farm at Davis, California. These seedlings are now
being transplanted to about 1,600 acres or 2,000
acres here, and some of them are being shipped to
Mexico to be planted there.

SEED—There is about 24,000 pounds of seed on
hand—1,000 pounds to be shipped to Mexico and
1,000 pounds discarded as being over-age.

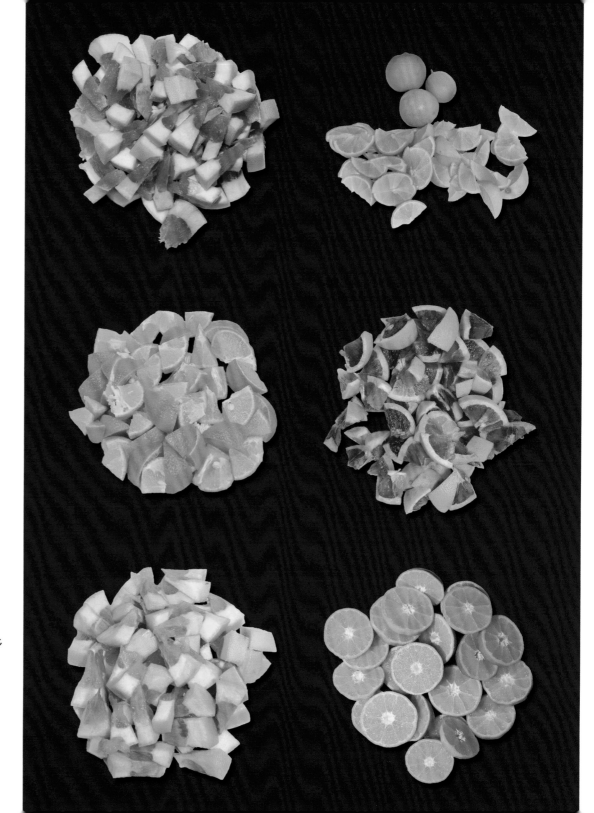

Selections, Citrus Fruit Tasting, Lindcove Research & Extension Center, University of California, 2006, Peter Goin. *[Clockwise from top left: Chandler pummelo, Thornless Mexican lime V, Moro blood orange, Tango mandarin, Rubidoux pummelo #1, and Michal mandarin.]*

BANC DIG 2017.14:Ag01334

Moro Blood Orange, Annual Grower's Citrus Tasting, Lindcove Research Center, University of California, 2006, Peter Goin.

BANC DIG 2017.14:Ag00521

Selections, Citrus Fruit Tasting, Lindcove Research & Extension Center, University of California

There's a tendency to think of citrus as citrus: all of a piece. That's unwise. First of all, citrus varieties are interfertile and hybridize readily. What is the new best thing one year can be yesterday's news a half-decade later. Second, citrus was domesticated perhaps 3,000 years ago, so there's been plenty of time for genetic variation to come around. Finally, novel varieties are literally market-changing. Such was the case with the seedless Bahia (or Washington, or Riverside) navel orange. Discovered in Brazil about 1820, early versions went to Australia and to USDA experimental gardens in Maryland. In 1870, twelve budded navel orange saplings were shipped to Riverside, where Eliza Tibbets received one, establishing the Parent Washington Navel Tree. By 1881, a million and a half orange trees were planted across Los Angeles County. While backyard trees are still common, the Southland's commercial crop acreage is way down since the 1950s. New varieties keep coming in the San Joaquin Valley, however: Cara Cara Pink Navels; Vaniglia Sanguigno; Bergamot, Buddha's hand, citron and clementines, Cuties and Kaffir limes, Meiwa kumquats and Tango or W. Murcott mandarins and Meyer lemons; the Satsuma and tangelo and Yuzu. If the names and different fruit types are an elaborate story, so too is cultivation and the clever breeding and cultivation handled by Agricultural Experiment Station personnel—and by commercial citrus growers. All have a stake in citrus success.

Moro Blood Orange, Annual Grower's Citrus Tasting, Lindcove Research Center

The Moro blood orange is particularly flamboyant, with subtle gradational shadings to its internal color that make it sought after for juice or eating; seen here at Lindcove Citrus Food Tasting and Display Field Day, Tulare County.

A discovery in Sicily in the fifteenth century, the supply of blood oranges was marshaled and cultivated and made its way elsewhere in Italy, to Spain, and finally, to California. Its hue and pause-giving color make blood orange sorbet a favorite, along with considerable demand in traditional Seville marmalade. The fruit, after being outré for a time, is resoundingly back in fashion, and seen in fine restaurants and carefully added to salads and desserts.

Gamboni Farming Company, Dos Palos, Merced County

A modest yet iconic building owned by Gamboni Farming in Dos Palos, Merced County, hardly communicates any sense of an agribusiness venture that received nearly $3.5 million dollars in federal subsidy payments from 1995–2016, largely paid to cotton producers (or in some cases, to growers who hold back on planting). According to the Environmental Working Group's Farm Subsidy Database and the USDA, Gamboni Farming Co. received payments totaling $3,493,871 from 1995 through 2016. They were far from the largest. Farmer's Rice Cooperative, in Sacramento, received $149 million, 1995–2016; Dublin Farms in Corcoran $21 million; Hansen Ranches (also Corcoran) took in $16 million; Buttonwillow Land and Cattle, the same amount. "Subsidies" may sound like a disapproving term; it helps to know that just 9.2% of California farms received a federal subsidy in 2007 (comparative data is not current but this offers a contrast). The so-called "specialty crops" of California set the state apart. In North Dakota, 83% of farms received subsidies; 81% of Iowa farms, and the total amount disbursed nationwide was $349 billion.

Gamboni Farming Company, Dos Palos, Merced County, 2007, Peter Goin.

BANC DIG 2017.14:Ag01049

Bee, Yellow and Purple Blossom, Cotton Field, Merced County

Cotton is a fascinating crop. On a dusty dirt road near Merced a field might beckon with pink, white, and yellow flowers. Here was no flowerland nursery. Over the course of a walk into the middle of the crop, nothing seemed distinctive or definitive. Suspicion grows: small cardboard boxes, hard to see, turn out to be labeled "boll weevil traps." At hand is the answer: the crop was cotton, through and through, but before the bolls began to appear, and weeks before they would be sprayed with a defoliant to remove vexing foliage, leaving behind just cotton: a sea of stems and puffy cotton bolls.

Hand Holding Cotton Cloud at Harvested Field, Merced County

Hand-held cotton bolls, supported above a defoliated cotton field in Merced County, speak to the scale of cotton production in the San Joaquin Valley, where cotton (both upland and American-Pima) are sizable economic contributors to farm-gate value.

Cotton Loaf Destined for Dos Palos Cooperative Gin

Viewed from the side, there appears to be a twelve-foot tall wall blasted by cotton balls. The perception is not so far off. While cotton harvesting is much changed in California from the backbreaking stoop labor of the 1950s and '60s, mechanized harvesters produce enormous bread-loaves the size of semi-trucks of densely packed cotton bolls that still require processing through a cotton gin to remove seeds and impurities. The longer-staple and the organic cotton increasingly favored by California growers is not immune from the ginning requirement, and with decreasing numbers of gins, the delays are often longer, with this cotton covered in protective plastic as growers wait for prices to rise and ginning costs to settle.

Bee, Yellow and Purple Blossom, Cotton Field, Merced County, 2006, Peter Goin.

BANC DIG 2017.14:Ag00150

Hand Holding Cotton Cloud at Harvested Field, Merced County, 2007, Peter Goin.

Cotton Loaf Destined for Dos Palos Cooperative Gin, 2007, Peter Goin.

Horse Drawn Combine

Machinery is crucial. Grain harvests changed with adoption of the grain combine in the Midwest and Great Plains of the late 1800s, but it was equipment perfected in California. Describing that crucial and costly device as a "combine" was significant because just one piece of machinery was required to reap, thresh, and winnow grain, three steps that in earlier days required a crew of literally dozens of hired farm hands. The combine was beastly heavy and was drawn by up to twenty draft horses. The combine machinery was powered by a bullwheel, using a technology similar to early oil drilling operations that was turned by the forward motion of the horse-drawn combine wheels. Then in 1911, Stockton's Holt Manufacturing Company created an engine that could power the processing of wheat or other grains: it could eliminate the labor of a dozen farmhands. No less important was breaking ground for cultivation: The crawler tractor was created by the California's Stockton Wheel Service, established in 1892, which in no time was producing dozers or treaded tractors (as opposed to wheeled), used to harvest grain under the Holt company name. The crawler tractor (or dozer) wide tread area in contact with the ground was a boon for drawing huge equipment across loosened soil and treaded machinery compacts soil less than conventional tractor tires. In 1925, Holt Manufacturing would merge with a competitor to become the Caterpillar Tractor Company. Caterpillar is today a continuing and dominant worldwide source for heavy equipment used in farming, mining, construction, road building, loading, excavation, logging, grading, and truck-based transportation.

Horse Drawn Combine, 1920–1930, Photograph Department of Holt Manufacturing Co., Stockton, California.

Agriculture and Flood-Related Photographs from the Miller & Lux Collection.

BANC PIC 1973.056—PIC folders 1

Afron Dual Boom Topper / Hedger; World Ag Expo, Tulare, 2006, Peter Goin.

Big G Greenline Five-Section Disc, World Ag Expo, Tulare, 2006, Peter Goin.

Afron Dual Boom Topper / Hedger; World Ag Expo, Tulare

Not something out of *Star Wars* or an '80s slasher film, the arms of this massive tree pruning device are used to carve and trim the sides of trees in an orchard to make it possible for cultivators and harvesters to travel between the rows. A similar machine will flattop pear, orange, and other tree crops to keep them at a manageable height where workers can climb safely to harvest the crop. Edward Scissorhands would grow green with envy.

Big G Greenline Five-Section Disc, World Ag Expo, Tulare

A Big G Green Line HD 5000 Series Five-Section Double Offset Disc, when mated to a crawler tractor of sufficient drawbar horsepower can cover 30—35 acres per hour. Size does not necessarily come at the cost of agility: It takes three minutes for the hydraulics to fold the 60-foot wide unit to a highway-ready width of 16 feet, 6 inches. The sight would stir the soul of any five-year-old boy—and many a comparably aged girl. Deep sandy soils in the San Joaquin and Sacramento valleys often have hardpans at depth below the surface, a feature that is a natural product of caliche (calcium carbonate layers) or brought on by repeated tillage. That hardpan needs to be broken up before establishing almond groves, vineyards, or other crops. The process involves deep ripping, which shatters the hardpan layer, and makes possible the addition of various soil amendments like fertilizers, gypsum, potash, and lime. "Ripping" soil is not easy, however. Rippers (and sometimes a single claw-like tine, ten or more feet long) are drawn behind a crawler tractor, often a D7 or D8 or larger Caterpillar dozer, to break up the subsoil and its compacted hardpan. That slow process is only step one. Next comes disking, to break large chunks of soil into smaller pieces, and a third stage uses laser-directed soil planes or levelers than make a field ready for planting. Further pre-planting expenses involve trellising or building wide pads for planting. The costs involved in field preparation are predictably large—and incurred before planting a single seed or grafted grape or a sapling or bare-root tree.

Alfalfa 6 ft. 2 in. high; oats nearly 6 ft. high

Innovation is not all about the business side of things. Farmers accustomed to a certain crop productivity have always found unusual exceptions in California, whether dairy cows that take to an open system of overhead shelters and a generous milking regime or genteel farmers reveling in the production of alfalfa or oats. Soil fertility and plant fecundity can reign victorious. The geographer James J. Parsons kept a ten-foot-tall stalk of *Avena fatua*, a strand of California wild oats, next to his living room fireplace, simply because it was startlingly and aberrantly tall.

Date Palms, Coachella Valley, California

The palm is such a characteristic California "tree" (it's really not a tree by conventional botanical descriptions, technically it's a grass). There were native palms in California, but those are concentrated in desert canyons in eastern San Diego, Imperial, and Riverside counties. The generous canopy and the old world flavor of palm production (coconut— rare; date palm—still regularly found) caught the attention of photographers, and both Dorothea Lange and Ansel Adams created memorable images of date palms in full health and production.

Alfalfa 6 ft. 2 in. high; oats nearly 6 ft. high, 1910–1915, McCurry Foto Company, San Francisco, Gelatin silver print.

From album Rivergarden Farm.

BANC PIC 1977.019:60

Date Palms, Coachella Valley, California, 1937, Dorothea Lange. FSA-OWI

Farm Security Administration photograph collection [graphic].

BANC PIC 1942.008 (multiple boxes)

Wrapped Palms in Mecca, Riverside County

Fire up Google Earth on the computer and zoom in on Indio, in eastern Riverside County, and this scene is immediately recognizable, reproduced a dozen or a hundred times. Native palms in California are rare: Just one variety, _Washingtonia filifera_ is endemic to desert canyons in the Southland and in Baja. Imported palms, however, came early with visitors from afar. Paintings of Mission San Diego de Alcalá executed in the 1850s by artists such as Edward Vischer show exotic palm varieties planted near the original eighteenth-century buildings; little wonder that later photographers including Dorothea Lange and Ansel Adams favored palm trees as subjects in their work. And today ornamental palms still mark the location of many a prosperous farm-house—some occupied, others relict—as far north as Colusa, in the northern Sacramento Valley. In this view, recently transplanted palm specimens in Mecca, California, are still wrapped to prevent sun damage to growing points atop their trunks.

Wrapped Palms in Mecca, Riverside County, 2007, Peter Goin.

Palm Trees and House, North of Salinas, Monterey County, 2010, Peter Goin.

Sequence of Olive Harvest, 2009, Peter Goin.

Olive Harvester, 2009, Peter Goin.

Palm Trees and House, North of Salinas, Monterey County
At the terminus of a slender driveway in the Salinas Valley, flanked by topiary on one side and paralleled on the other road verge by a commercial strawberry crop neatly transplanted into plastic-covered rows, are twin palms and a handsome farmhouse fashioned in the Queen Anne-style. Active agriculture in the late nineteenth century attracted families of status and some wealth. As fortunes improved, growers (they had graduated to that designation from being "farmers") built houses in town or on their farm sites in the countryside that they felt would be appropriate statements of their aspirations and success. In big Ag centers—Colusa, Modesto, Porterville, Winters, Visalia—the fortunes made in farming, ranching, and merchandising associated with agriculture made entire districts of elegant homes routine. It's always easy to recognize where the old money households established their community presence. A hundred years after fortunes were made from farming or equipment sales or ranching, the homes remain but the resident families are not the same. The finest Victorian-era homes are now often converted to offices for law firms or doctors. But in most cases, the first money came from farming.

Sequence of Olive Harvest... Olive Harvester
The olive harvester (adapted from technology originally used to harvest berries and other trellised crops) seems to consume trees that are carefully trained along smooth wires, and topped to keep them under six and a half feet. Trained along wires in the fashion of espaliered orchard trees, the olives grow under a regimen of carefully administered drip irrigation, fertilizer, gypsum, and other soil-enhancing inputs. After the machine harvester passes by, left behind is a scattering of broken branches, a few uncaptured olives that were shaken from the espaliered trees, and a great improvised machine receding into the distance. In Spain or Portugal or Italy or Greece, which is to say, the northern Mediterranean Basin, twenty trees per acre would require hours of time from a harvesting crew. But in these new plantings, machinery reduces labor by ninety percent, and oil quality is said to go undiminished. The consortium that developed California Olive Ranch is, curiously enough, a group of Spaniards, and the technology used is bit-by-bit spreading to Chile, Australia, South Africa, and—of course—to the Iberian Peninsula. With labor in short supply, mechanization is an innovation that can truly add to efficiency.

Distinctive Extra-Virgin Olive Oil, Emerging from the State-of-the-art Press at California Olive Ranch
The end result is a green-golden flow. Spain and Portugal have, for a number of years, been engaged in a battle-royal with Italian producers of extra virgin olive oil. The legal dockets of the European Union are flush with complaints where Spanish olive growers argue that Italian producers have played an unfair game: labeling oil from other parts of the Mediterranean fringe as "Italian"—and therefore eligible for classification under EU "denomination of origin" classifications. Californian producers have readily played into the controversy and laid their own claim to fair-market production. Certainly, the end result is fetching, although as of 2016, only 2% of the olive oil consumed in the United States was grown in the U.S., and virtually all of that was a California product.

Distinctive Extra-Virgin Olive Oil, Emerging from the State-of-the-art Press at California Olive Ranch, 2009, Peter Goin.

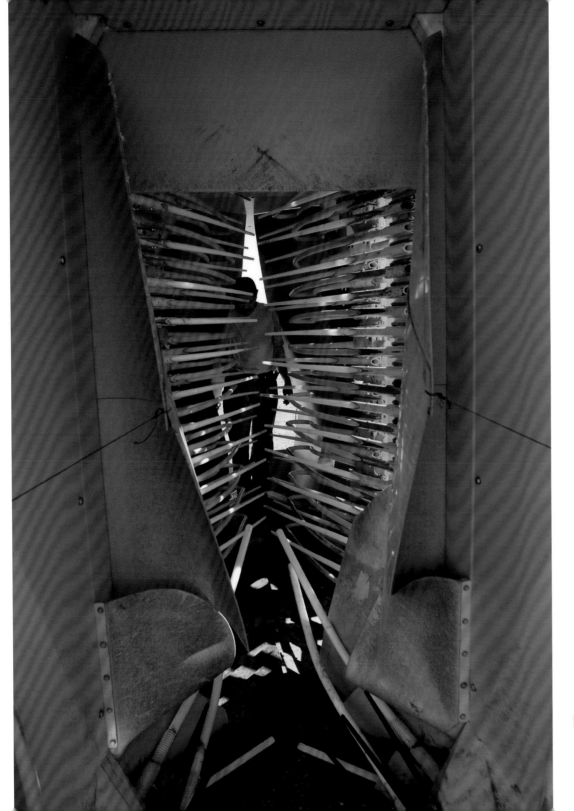

Harvesting Machine for Olives: View within Teeth Area
The formidable maw of a mechanical harvester intimidates
the untutored observer. At the California Olive Ranch
near Gridley, a Gregoire Model 167 is adapted to harvest
ultra-high-density plantings of olives, grown on trellises,
that are planted with up to 700 trees per acre—a marked
contrast to the traditional olive tree density of 20–40 stems
per acre. What seem to be scary "teeth" are actually nylon
straight rods designed to penetrate deeper into the olive
canopy to knock loose up to 95% of the olives, far more
than might be gleaned by other mechanical harvesters. In a
few seconds, a tree can be stripped of fruit; it would take a
human picking crew a quarter hour or more, working as a
team, to get the same results—and these days, such a labor
supply is notoriously difficult to find and hire. Legends of
the American southeast and published folklore indices (for
example Stith Thompson (F547.1)), are full of references
to such toothed apparitions—delicacy prevents long-form
discussion, but much was blamed on Sigmund Freud.

Harvesting Machine for Olives: View within Teeth Area, 2009, Peter Goin.

BANC DIG 2017.14:AgAg01164

ROMANCE

IS THERE ROMANCE TO AGRICULTURE? NARY A DOUBT, AND ALONG WITH THAT COMES MYTHOLOGY AND IDEALIZED LANDSCAPES AND MARKETING. If plants can succumb to romance—a bee or hummingbird or wasp or even a wisp of pollinating breeze is the intermediary—then perhaps an engagingly arranged and photographed seed catalogue is the equivalent of the food-fancier's wish list. On occasion there is torrid sex, of course, since so much of what is eaten owes everything to the vigorous reproduction of plants and animals. In eating, much of the attraction is in the mind, imagined. Consider what the food stocks were like five or six hundred years ago, wherever our ancestors hailed from. Variety was rare, and through passage of the seasons, winter into spring especially, the larder would look less and less welcoming and definitely wanting. Ethnotaxonomist Gary Paul Nabhan and novelist Barbara Kingsolver set about assessing local foods—setting a distance from home and trying to make 80 or 90 percent of what each of them ate and fed their family come from within that radius. That made "following your food" at least theoretically possible, especially if a part of the process was going someplace to pick a specific item, or meet the grower, or to harvest wild foods, or snare or shoot game. There's an element of choice, reason, confidence and control, and familiarity (and romance) in eating what you grow, pick, or seek out.

Because lands with a Mediterranean-type, summer-dry climate can grow so many crops, California drew the curious, with its open spaces of seemingly-available land. Native American populations would grind acorns, eat birds after netting, and wild plants after gathering. Along the California coast, they knew their resources and consumed shellfish and fisheries products, from steelhead salmon to the white sturgeon that frequent waters of San Pablo Bay. Many sturgeon today are caught and released, and they now must be under a maximum size. Just as well, since in 2011, a twelve-foot long 1,000 pound white sturgeon was weighed and released, and a 1,500 pound specimen was allegedly caught in the upper Sacramento River in the 1880s, where it was hauled out by a team of horses. There was much food to be had. In plenty there is security, and in security, romance.

Varied eras arose in California. Early on came gathering: wild bird eggs from the Farallon Islands and oysters from Bay waters; livestock harvested from the grasslands and range of the Spanish—Mexican era ranchos. Those produced a modest income in hides and rendered tallow, which went to light urban surrounds and households. Arriving Gold Rush populations ran through available supplies of food quickly, and for a time, wild game had to meet demand until long market drives brought cattle from Mexico and the American Southwest. By the 1880s, coming to California and getting involved in crop growing was a draw, as cities arose and discerning tastes with them. A later boom was found in more processed products, especially grapes, another introduction by Dominican and Franciscan friars, who liked their wine and fortified spirits. A boom was generated that, with a pause during Prohibition, truly hasn't left. And finally, the crop of the moment, subject to a chaos of marketing and consumption and regulation, is without a doubt cannabis, which however you spin the figures is likely the most valuable crop in California today.

As an emblem, consider the saga of the orange tree. Oranges offer a bouquet of blossoms, fruit, and an added virtue that oranges can be left on the tree without spoilage, so long as there is no hard freeze, to be picked when the market is best. Well into the 1950s, California offered orange towns, orange festivals, orange shows, orange groves, and, of course, orange fruit. The essence of California was boxed and sent to the whole country. Easterners and midwesterners would eat oranges, experiencing "The Golden State" vicariously. Yet nationally, diet changed; consumption of oranges in the United States rose from no oranges per capita in 1890 to 40 oranges per American in 1914. In a sense, it was California itself being sold. One of the more famous labels shows Uncle Sam, an orange in hand, with the text: "I grow these myself in California." The response was welcoming. It was a romance—of a fruit and all it symbolized.

Shields Date Gardens Sign Advertising "The Romance and Sex Life of the Date in Sound & Color," 2007, Peter Goin.

BANC DIG 2017.14:Ag00622

Shields Date Gardens Sign Advertising "The Romance and Sex Life of the Date in Sound & Color"

In existence for just under a hundred years, the Shields Date Gardens in Indio, California, remains a go-to destination, and generations of Southern Californians and long-haul visitors remember acquiring a date shake at the counter and wandering the store counters, absorbing and considering the slightly crunchy yet sweet texture and taste, and perhaps catching the film: "Romance and Sex Life of the Date." If now quaint, in its original form probably it was even a bit racy for travelers making the long 1930s haul across Route 66, the Mother Road, from the Dust Bowl to Riverside and Imperial counties, and other more verdant parts of California where there was a promise of jobs and housing.

Hanford, Kings County, California: The Richest Spot in the San Joaquin Valley, "The Garden of the Sun"

Kings County was not among the earliest or most prosperous counties in interior California, but certainly it has changed with time, its river waters diverted, and lake sediments retasked for agricultural use. A degree of boosterism was normal, in presentations of self, but this brochure from 1921 is exceptionally cheerful, promising "You'll like Hanford." Its advertised charms include varied crops, a growing population, "attractive, well-stocked stores and shops and wide-awake progressive merchants." A special come-on is the penultimate boastful paragraph: "No earthquakes, no cyclones, no blizzards, no snow, no bad winds, no electric

storms, no humidity." This was a degree of self-promotion by no means unusual in the San Joaquin and Sacramento valleys; it played to an agricultural and industrial strong hand, especially where transportation and the production of oil and natural gas was concerned. An upbeat spirit can be good. Unmentioned at the time were observed but unidentified southern San Joaquin maladies like endemic Valley fever (Coccidioidomycosis), with pneumonia-like respiratory distress symptoms associated with a virulent soil-based fungus delivered by airborne dust. Charles E. Smith, whose work on *Coccidioides immitis* began at Stanford, in 1951 would leave the Stanford "Farm" to become dean of UC Berkeley's School of Public Health.

California Eve Oranges; Home Brand (R.A. Eddy); Landscape Brand (Alta-Cresta Citrus Association); Nightcap Brand (Anaheim Community Growers)

At once magnet, tourist attraction, and moneymaker, California's orange groves offered what the historian Richard Lillard once dubbed a "picture postcard reality." Like a postcard, orange crate labels not only recorded a time and a place, they touted Southern California's attributes, obvious in this selection of four labels produced using a stone-lithography technique perfected by the Schmidt Lithograph Company of San Francisco. Custom-designed to an orange grove owner's specifications, orange crate labels—by some estimates two billion of them—were affixed to stout wooden crates from the 1870s through the mid-1950s, when cardboard sadly replaced wood. Images of California, presented to a wider American public at the start of the twentieth century, helped bring legions of tourists, and soon migrants, to the Golden State. Crate labels might promote views of California more fanciful than frank, reinforcing a hyperbolic ideal. But always there was truth enough to spark recognition in a larger public.

California's draw of the 1850s was gold, the pursuit of which forged a trail of mining enthusiasts from San Francisco Bay to the Sierra Nevada foothills. Looking for a nugget was a gamble, a search for something by its nature both elusive and exclusive. Orange growing, as the gold boom's successor, was much more democratic. The orange grove was attainable; anyone could in theory become an orange grower. That, precisely, was part of its attractiveness. A society as dramatically urbanized as contemporary California sometimes forgets that raising agricultural crops develops special connotations and prestige. Essentially Californian, "Orange Culture" was everything impossible back home, the perfect symbol of a new, a California, way of life. After World War II, oranges began disappearing from large parts of Southern California, and so faded an era of the genteel hobbyist farmer. With the idealized resident-citrus grower gone, the citrus industry in California moved north and east. Larger-scale growers instead sought out acreage in Tulare, Kern, and Fresno counties. A central point in California agricultural promoter Edward Wickson's writing and citrus evangelizing was simple—small-scale agriculture and ranching were more than economic pursuits; they offered a life of social and cultural significance. Little wonder Wickson (1848–1923) became both Dean of Berkeley's College of Agriculture and director of the Agricultural Experiment Station until his retirement in 1912, though he continued as emeritus professor of horticulture until his death in 1923.

THE CITY OF HANFORD HAS

pF869 H3A2

6,500 POPULATION. (COUNTY 25,000).

Four strong banks, commercial and savings.

Two daily newspapers, Hanford Morning Journal and Hanford Daily Sentinel (evening).

Attractive, well-stocked stores and shops and wide-awake, progressive merchants.

New $500,000 high school group as central feature of excellent and modern school system.

City and county library of 60,000 volumes.

Your church and your favorite lodge.

Headquarters for one of the largest and most active County Farm Bureaus in the state.

More than 10 miles of city paved streets, connecting with 110-mile system of county paved highways and main state highway trunk lines.

Gas, electricity and the finest, purest, softest artesian domestic water in the world.

Average annual rainfall of 8.40 inches.

Average mean annual temperature 62.2 degrees.

Mild, delightful winter climate; warm, healthful summers, with a never-failing breeze that makes summer nights a delight.

No earthquakes, no cyclones, no blizzards, no snow, no bad winds, no electric storms, no humidity.

You'll like Hanford.

HANFORD
KINGS COUNTY
CALIFORNIA

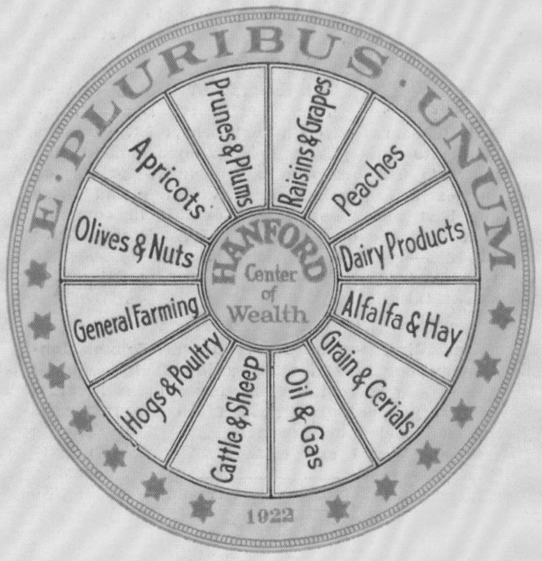

THE RICHEST SPOT IN THE
SAN JOAQUIN VALLEY
"THE GARDEN OF THE SUN"

FOR FURTHER INFORMATION WRITE
HANFORD BOARD OF TRADE
HANFORD, CALIFORNIA

Hanford, Kings County, California: The Richest Spot in the San Joaquin Valley, "The Garden of the Sun," ca. 1921.

BANC Pamphlet, pF869.H3A2

*California Eve Oranges; Home Brand
(R.A. Eddy). Schmidt Lithograph
Company records*, [1912–1929]. Two
views of Schmidt Lithograph orange crate
labels from company record sample books.

BANC NC MSS 67/171

Landscape Brand (Alta-Cresta Citrus Association); Nightcap Brand (Anaheim Community Growers). Schmidt Lithograph Company records, [1912–1929]. Two views of Schmidt Lithograph orange crate labels from company record sample books.

BANC NC MSS 67/171

Fruits of California Dessert Apricots

Can labels offered a fruitful vision of California: "Fruits of California," in this case, "dessert apricots" of "superior quality" and in "heavy syrup." All hailing from San Jose, then the fruit mecca of California. That was before its stone fruit producers and truck farmers were displaced by wartime relocation, a hunger for housing, and, after the early 1960s, by the feverish rise of Silicon Valley. This label art includes two grizzly bears fighting off a rampaging eagle that, talons extended, is attacking a container adorned with this same label—brand reinforcement at its finest. The fruits on the left side of the label are less militant: pears, peaches, plums, strawberries, cherries, and apricots. Labels for fruit and vegetables were a growth industry, a printing-house profit maker.

The California Beauty

Subtlety isn't the right word to describe labels for fruit and vegetable containers. The "California Beauty" is an image of feminine beauty and youth, bounteous, yet chaste and restrained. The allure of California fruit growing is fully addressed by the eyes of the protagonist in this Currier & Ives lithograph. A ruffle at her neck, a garland of grapes resting on tightly-curled hair, this winsome charmer is, by the standards of her age, indeed "The California Beauty." She is not promised to anyone who comes to California, but there is an aura of attainability, a different kind of romance.

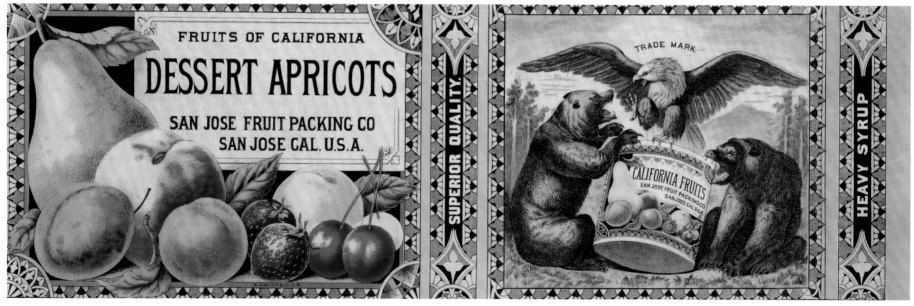

Fruits of California Dessert Apricots. Schmidt Lithograph Company records [1912–1929].

THE CALIFORNIA BEAUTY.

PUBLISHED BY CURRIER & IVES 152 NASSAU ST. NEW YORK.

The California Beauty, Currier & Ives. Lithograph on paper. Robert B. Honeyman, Jr. Collection of Early Californian and Western American Pictorial Material.

BANC PIC 1963.002:0815—B

Potato Carnival in Stockton, Alice Knudsen as Queen

Carnivals and crop fairs are events that tie together products, their growers, and an eating audience, and those ancient traditions are thoroughly bound up with a community's equinoctial harvest festival. Can celebration of a bountiful crop, of a diminishing daily routine of tilling and gleaning, and filling larders and granaries have a name? The celebration is what in Hawaii is called "pau hana," the end of the work day and a release from duties. For California, the festivals and rituals plug into a romance of agriculture. Having a signature crop brings a community a certain cachet, particularly resonant in an era before social media, 24/7 news cycles, vaunted self-promoters, and reality television. Granted, being named the Potato Queen of Tracy and showcased in a parade in nearby Stockton wasn't necessarily a towering privilege, but Alice Knudsen and her princesses have that look of pageant pros in this 1924 photograph. The platform is modest, compared to the elaborate rose-covered floats of the Rose Parade. Advertised in paint on a side panel is "prosperity for all seasons," a theme any booster of farming might salute, and the float is passing under the network of wires used by the Stockton electric interurban railways (the competing Stockton Electric Railroad and the Central California Traction Company).

Potato Carnival in Stockton, Alice Knudsen as Queen, 1924, Unknown photographer.

Gelatin silver print. Earle E. Williams photograph collection.

BANC PIC 1986.051—fALB:96

Dairy Princesses, World Ag Expo, Tulare, California, 2006, Peter Goin.

Dairy Princesses

A celebration of agriculture by giving it "princesses" and "queens" has deep roots in folklore. In California, for example, Marilyn Monroe in 1947 was the first Miss California Artichoke Queen in Castroville, California, which was then, and is still, self-proclaimed as the Artichoke Capital of the World. Showcasing an entire dairy princess court, the epic-scale annual World Ag Expo in Tulare offers a testament to the dominance of California's dairy industry, which is particularly concentrated in Fresno and Tulare counties. Events that celebrate dairy producers and offer line workers a chance to let off weekend steam are frequent. Perhaps no single group is so devoted to festivals as the San Joaquin Valley's dairy owners. A great many of them have family origins in Portugal—or the distant Azores, which provided an early workforce for dairy labor. Even there is a story: More than a few of the Azoreans who came to run tuna fleets out of San Diego, or worked in northern California dairies, are today dairy owners, though Dutch surnames are common too in the dairying world. There are rotating religious-flavored events around Central Valley towns, serving Portuguese and Mexican populations. Thornton, a small town in San Joaquin County, hosts a particularly important gathering, the *Festa* of the Holy Ghost associated with the Our Lady of Fatima, held yearly. Bread is distributed to all spectators (along with small cartons of milk), a priest blesses the dairy cows, handlers are dwarfed by a parade of giant oxen, girls promenade in elaborate white dress finery, each long veil and train protected from the ground by a carefully-cut plastic shield. Wrapping up the revelry is a bloodless bullfight, a communal meal, and a celebratory outdoor mass. At this somewhat less chaotic setting in Tulare, these young women represent a different kind of an overarching community sponsor, the California Milk Advisory Board.

Chinese Shell Peddlers, Monterey, California, 1890s. Miscellaneous California Views.

BANC PIC 1905.12811—PIC

Oyster in Black Rubber Glove with Tomales Bay in Background;
Hog Island Oyster Company, Marin County, 2006, Peter Goin.

Chinese Shell Peddlers, Monterey, California

Big abalone shells, necklaces, and an enterprising group of young Chinese vendors are working a stand in Monterey. Like the abalone itself, they fit into a larger story. There is evidence that Chumash Indians used abalone shells for adornment and exchange—in effect, as money—along the southern coast of California, and the Channel Islands have Native American abalone shell middens. With sizable late nineteenth-century abalone populations in coastal Santa Barbara and San Diego, harvest for commercial purposes was a Chinese initiative, as this stand suggests. Fisheries archives for 1879 record a harvest of abalone shells totaling 500,000 pounds. Little wonder that, by 1900, although abalone as a delicacy persisted, stocks were seriously depleted. In 1915, the state of California outlawed the export of abalone meat to China where it was considered a delicacy (and is farmed there, today). Technically marine snails, abalone grow in handsome iridescent shells that are often collected and dried for use as garden ornaments or mother-of-pearl, and often turned into buttons, jewelry, inlay, and buckles. Nor is the pursuit of abalone easy, since they live below the high tide line, often under rock overhangs; the rock-picker will work with an abalone iron carrying a gauge to make sure any taken are above the minimum size, and in 2017 the limit was reduced to twelve abalone per year. Abalone prefer cold water environments, which adds to the challenge of harvest; every year a handful of abalone harvesters off the California coast perish because of various mishaps, and access to abalone-dense sites is often restricted by coastal landowners. Scuba gear is prohibited, and some of the casualties come with free divers working at a depth of thirty feet or more. Poaching is a problem, too, and check-stations set up along north coast roads capture illegally caught abalone—with accompanying hefty fines or arrest.

Oyster in Black Rubber Glove with Tomales Bay in Background; Hog Island Oyster Company, Marin County

While not an obvious agricultural crop, oysters are produced in several locations in California. Backed by Tomales Bay, in Marin County, this striking Hog Island Oyster Company specimen is an example of *Crassostrea gigas*, the Pacific oyster. Once the entire San Francisco Bay Area was a huge producer of oyster, mussels, shrimp, and other shellfish. And they were a staple for the Native American population. In the East Bay was the Emeryville Shellmound, 60 feet high and some 350 feet in diameter. By 1999, final remnants of the shellmound were demolished to permit construction of a shopping mall. The historic refuse midden site was an archeological wonderland documenting eating habits of the area's once-sizable Ohlone or Costanoan Native American population. Nor was the consumption of oysters, clams, cockles, and mussels solely an Ohlone practice. From the Gold Rush era onward, eating oysters was as much a symbol of prosperity as a ready source of protein. Oysters were eaten in better restaurants across northern California, and actually went by train in the 1910s to Nevada gold and silver-mining towns, carefully settled in chipped ice, yet delivered (so the promise went) within twenty-four hours of harvest. The career of the independent oysterman was endangered by sediment washed westward by hydraulic monitors used in gold mining operations in the Sierra Nevada, which carried slurry down the Sacramento River, choked the Delta, and silted significant parts of San Francisco Bay. Oyster production all but collapsed, though there are attempts to restart a bayside industry. Political events and recent conservation controversies have taken an added toll on Bay Area oyster farms. Termination in 2011 of the Drakes Bay Oyster Company lease within Point Reyes National Seashore generated heated and sometimes friendship-ending controversy in Marin County, and reduced oyster production in California by nearly two-thirds. Closure of all operations in 2014 is a reminder that today choices are required to sustain agriculture in an overwhelmingly urban California.

Close-up of Interior of Purple Cabbage, San Benito County, 2006, Peter Goin.

BANC DIG 2017.14:Ag00405

White Caps, on Frisee Lettuce Star Route Farm, Bolinas, 2006, Peter Goin.

BANC DIG 2017.14:Ag00213

Close-up of Interior of Purple Cabbage ... White Caps,
on Frisee Lettuce

Among the joys of traveling side roads with the
companionship of fruit trees and field plantings is an
absorbing pleasure in seeing the crops themselves.
Whether emergent seedlings or nearly harvestable, they
have their own kind of romance, maybe a little prurient or
at least suggestive. Over there is a purple cabbage—wait,
no, a whole field of them—so reminiscent of a Georgia
O'Keefe painting. Stop, admire, give a shake of the head,
laugh, and drive on. Evocative white caps protect and
shape frisée, a form of curly endive sometimes known
as chicory, grow neatly covered in Bolinas.

Hand-held Honeydew Melon, Sutter County, 2006, Peter Goin.

BANC DIG 2017.14:Ag00127

Two Persimmons with Branches, near Exeter, Tulare County, 2006, Peter Goin.

BANC DIG 2017.14:Ag00556

Close-up of Kiwi Cluster, Live Oak, Sutter County, 2006, Peter Goin.

BANC DIG 2017.14:Ag00119

Large Faux Orange and Roadside Stand, 2006, Peter Goin.

Hand-held Honeydew Melon... Two Persimmons with Branches... Close-up of Kiwi Cluster... Large Faux Orange

Monumentality is an important part of producer self-image. Here a giant orange; there an awesome apple. Pride goeth before a fall, but grower pride in product and place is commemorated across California, where "specialty crops" rule. There's dangling kiwifruit—brought in from the wilds of China to New Zealand by missionaries, then sent to Chico for test-planting where it met with success. A melon, gorgeous and firm. An orange, crafted of fiberglass, sitting meditatively on a surplus tire beside a fruit stand. And the always-exquisite persimmon, which often is stored on the tree long after all leaves are shed. The fortunes of amateur or professional fruit growers in California often were cemented by working even small acreages of productive and profitable crops. Of them all, the navel orange was queen, which from the late nineteenth-century onward drew devotees to Los Angeles, the Inland Empire, and the San Joaquin Valley. While never an inexpensive crop to establish, navel and Valencia oranges rewarded cultivation and together became icons of California's golden possibilities—enough to inspire roadside advertisements and attractants, such as this statue.

Cherry Cluster at U-pick Farm, Contra Costa County

Cherry trees are admired not just in Japan, but of course in the United States, and harvesting the fruit is a particularly delicate and labor-intensive activity. The fruit repays close inspection and admiration for their color, ripeness, and sheer delectability. Coming early in the stone-fruit harvest season, cherries are one of the crops that is most popular for U-pick farm visitors. The result of a visit can involve canning, pie-making, even a gift to friends and family.

Delon Deng and Eva Wu at U-pick, Brentwood, California

Pursuit of the freshest produce, the finery of spring, time outside, and a potential crop of fruit eaten by hand or canned can entice many and diverse visitors. There can even be romance in picking and choosing the best fruits of an early season, and convincing a friend or partner to partake of a spring visit to a U-pick farm site, where they can load up on fruit that will be a far sight fresher and more attractive than what might be found a week or two later in a store. Delon and Eva are taking a post-harvest break at Bacchini's Fruit Tree U-pick farm in Brentwood, eastern Contra Costa County.

Wrapped Organic Purple Cauliflower, Phil Foster Ranches, San Benito County, 2006, Peter Goin.

BANC DIG 2017.14:Ag 00400

Cherry Cluster at U-pick Farm, Contra Costa County, 2007, Peter Goin.

BANC DIG 2017.14:Ag00832

Delon Deng and Eva Wu at U-pick,
Brentwood, California, 2007, Peter Goin.

BANC DIG 2017.14:Ag00831

Demonstration Onion-processing Conveyor at World Ag Expo, Tulare, 2006, Peter Goin.

BANC DIG 2017.14:Ag00017

Organic Dried Hachiya Persimmon Slices, Ferry Plaza Farmer's Market, San Francisco, 2006, Peter Goin.

BANC DIG 2017.14:Ag 00242

Demonstration Onion-processing... Organic Dried Hachiya
Persimmon Slices... Wrapped Organic Purple Cauliflower
The processing, grading, and presentation involved in
California agricultural products generally takes place off-
farm, or at least off-field. It all counts as part of a complicated business: adding value to a crop and boosting its
allure. Whether organic, biodynamic, commercial-grade,
or off-label, sellable items are supposed to look good, and
a great deal of work goes into cosmetics and eye-catching
packaging. Some of it is mechanized, some is done by
hand. The results are what we look over, select from, and,
ultimately, eat. For some agricultural products, careful post-
harvest work, including clever marketing, can multiply value
by a factor of two or five or ten. Cellophane-bagged lettuce
and spinach are examples of a marketing scheme with a
niche and overall public acceptance in an age of ready-to-
eat convenience foods. At a higher price point, wine is a
good example. Red onions, persimmons—sliced and dried,
and the great cruciferous vegetable, cauliflower, each have
to go through an evaluation process before they are lifted off
of a shelf and transferred to a shopping cart for purchase.

Ostrich Farm, Pasadena

Among the varied products of California are startling
animal oddities, at least for the butcher's case: llamas,
alpacas, emu, yaks (yes), goose and duck eggs, rabbits.
Even ostriches. Long before emu-oil became a sought-after
product to heal cracked heels and ease away wrinkles, the
ostrich was embraced in odd parts of California as a valued
harvest. While today ostrich meat is praised as everything
that more thoroughly domesticated animals are not (white
meat, huge eggs, great at self-defense, low cholesterol), in
the early twentieth century, ostriches were all about feathers
and human decorations. *The Right Stuff*, the 1983 film
version (dir. Philip Kaufman) of Tom Wolfe's astronaut space
odyssey, includes a startling scene where the once-and-then-
again famous burlesque actress Sally Rand, to appearances
clad only in ostrich feathers, performs a fan dance before an
audience including Vice President Lyndon Johnson. Feather
fashions through the "flapper" era of the Roaring Twenties
found feather boas, hats, and other ornaments features of
great popularity, and in sites in Southern California and
the San Joaquin Valley (prominently so in Buttonwillow,
just north of the Grapevine) ostriches were a prominent
landscape feature, as recorded in *Feather Fashions and
Bird Preservation: A Study in Nature Protection*, published
by Robin Doughty in 1975 from his UC Berkeley doctoral
dissertation. To get those feathers, herds of live ostriches
were de rigueur, and they were a source of no small
fascination in California agriculture.

Ostrich Farm, Pasadena. Gelatin silver print. Miscellaneous California Views.

BANC PIC 1905.12803—PIC

Bagged and Labeled Peppers. Ferry Plaza Farmer's Market,
San Francisco, 2006, Peter Goin.

BANC DIG 2017.14:Ag00234

Olives, There for the Buying. Ferry Plaza Farmer's Market, San Francisco, 2006, Peter Goin.

BANC DIG 2017.14:Ag00235

Bagged and Labeled Peppers... Olives, There for the Buying...
Woman in Red with Cheeses

And in the end, agriculture comes down to the consumer: shopping, seeing, selecting, and—ultimately—serving. If the crop is alfalfa hay, then the consumer may be sheep, or goats, or horses, or cows, and if cows, they may be Californian, or almost as likely, Chinese, since containers that arrive in Oakland or Sacramento or at Long Beach, laden with Chinese goods, will often return stuffed with alfalfa pellets destined for Chinese dairies. Exports are important, with agricultural product exports earning more than a seventh of California's agricultural income. Not all is sheltered and shipped. It's at the supermarket deli counter, or these days at a farmers market, that more than a few sales are made, in a curious but pleasant return to the municipal market of bygone eras. The draw can involve taste testing and the pleasant anticipation of a snack or meal. An engaging presentation of cheeses (with crackers or baguettes to aid in consumption) draws the curious. For olives, the raw fruit, as picked from a tree, is loaded with oleuropein, a bitter compound that before eating has to be removed by one of several means of curing—water, brining, oil, salt, lye, with the added ingredient of time. The end result is tailored somewhat to the type of olive, and to how much effort someone is willing to devote to what can be a weeks-long process. More and more upscale groceries will offer potential buyers a dozen or more types of olives,

pitted or not, stuffed with garlic or pearl onions or blue cheese or pimento or lemon. Few regret the purchase. And a collection of peppers, small but in vivid living color, are available in net bags from a producer to your cloth shopping bag, in an easy motion. Is there romance to eating? Certainly so.

Souvenir of the Cawston Ostrich Farm, South Pasadena

The fashions themselves, including lofty items of women's haberdashery, were timely products of animal agriculture in the Golden State. While vanity may seem an odd contributor to agricultural production, fashion sense adds a certain continuity. After all, a savvy and select stream of early non-Native arrivals to California was in part shaped by visits from trappers who began arriving in 1784 and continued until an exploitable animal supply was exhausted. Europeans in droves—Spanish or French or American or British or Canadian—came and collected the fur, pelts, and

hides of sea and river mammals and their terrestrial kin. Along the northern coast of California, including Fort Ross and elsewhere, settlements were established by Russian trappers and traders. Over 35 years, the Russian-American Fur Company took some 100,000 sea otter pelts from Humboldt Bay to Baja California. What were they after? You name it: the skins of sea otter, fur seals, beaver pelts, gray fox, harbor seals, river otter, marten, and the elusive fisher. As it turned out, the mammals were trapped out so fast that only for a few decades was California a fur haven, but the profits to be had were formidable. At first, skins went across the Pacific to China where demand was great, and later around the Horn to New York and Europe. These products of what is sometimes called "commercial venery" would come back to the United States or be sold elsewhere as fashion ornaments, including belts, capes, clothes, and hats. Decades later, a trade in ostrich feathers offered women's fashions a taste of glamor and drama.

SPECIAL 1¾-yd. BOA, $20.00.

No. 204—Any Color. We are putting out this boa as a special inducement to our mail-order patrons, and endeavor to make it the finest ever sold anywhere for the price.

It is a fashionable length, 1¾ yards. It is made full and fluffy and is composed of the finest stock from the male ostriches' wings. This grade of feathers is the same as is used in fine plumes. It is a mistake to think we use inferior stock in our boas. This boa equals any that can be found in retail stores at $25.00, $27.50 or $30.00.

Delivered prepaid for...................................$20.00

OTHER SPECIAL BOAS.

No. 123—Ostrich Feather Boa is 1½ yards long, an excellent quality, but is not as heavy or fluffy as the boa described above. It is the best ever put out at the price, and is as good as retail stores sell for $18.00. It can be had in any color and will be delivered upon receipt of...................................$12.00

No. 255—Ostrich Feather Boa is two yards long and a finer quality than the $20.00 boa described above. It is heavier and longer. It is equally good value and is the best boa ever sold for the price. It can be had in black, white or any special shade dyed to order. Price, delivered, prepaid $25.00

Souvenir of the Cawston Ostrich Farm, South Pasadena, ca. 1906, Cawston Ostrich Farm.

BANC pF862.2.C45 1906

Woman in Red with Cheeses, The Cowgirl Creamery. Ferry Plaza Farmer's Market, San Francisco, 2006, Peter Goin.

Chinese Eggplant

A vegetable of the same family as tomatoes, potatoes, and peppers, *Solanum melongena* is rarely anyone's first and favorite vegetable—but appreciation can grow on you. Grill it under a shower of garlic; or batter, bread, and bake it Parmigiano style; stir fry, cube it into a tasty tempura batter, or slice your eggplant into raw rounds to eat by hand. And while we don't discuss the color "eggplant" much, the French name for the plant describes an elegant rich hue that color wonks refer to as Pantone hue 512, or describe the color card as simply "mid-aubergine." Farmers markets, Japanese grocery stores, greenhouses, grow and sell the toothsome crop, as here at San Francisco's biggest farmers market.

Chinese Eggplant, Ferry Plaza Farmer's Market, 2006, Peter Goin.

PAUL F. STARRS

ON THE ROAD AGAIN...

For years, I'd visited San Francisco Bay Area farming and livestock operations. My wife, a UC Berkeley professor, taught "Follow Your Food," culminating in a vast student-prepared meal, where they'd come into our house to prepare and eat what they'd acquired. A trip might send them to the dense produce sections in Oakland's Chinatown or Little Saigon. Or they'd take public transit to the Ferry Building Farmer's Market to meet Jessica Prentice, who coined the term "locavore." In a drive to Marin there were heirloom dwarf apple trees and calm Angus cattle waiting at Mike and Sally Gale's Chileno Valley Ranch. This all finally jelled: Here was a great story, visual and geographical, waiting to be told. A new story? Maybe not to growers and live-stock raisers—but less than 1% of Californians are involved in ag production. Even producers tend to know a small thing well, rarely taking in the entire picture. Restaurant critics lead fine lives, but rarely go to the source. Michael Pollan is wonderful, if more thoughtful and deliberative than a custodian of detailed facts. There was no field guide to agriculture, certainly not for California with its universe of crops and products. So we wrote one, working with words, facts, photographs, and maps — a *Field Guide to California Agriculture*.

After a project like this, with seven years of travel and recording before the *Field Guide* was in print and winning awards in 2010, our agricultural inquiries never hit an end. "I begin," the sage philosopher—farmer Wendell Berry writes, "with the proposition that eating is an agricultural act." Of course: Through time, we revise how we eat; what we consume changes. Whether growing older ourselves, or with children or grandchildren, we tweak our diet, departing from the mainstays, changing conceptions of shopping and cooking. Some finds are sheer luck: we learn from roadside stands, produce from a friend, opening a CSA box that puts different fare afore us. And periodically we enjoy a chance, if mind-bending, restaurant meal. Even the Internet with hundreds of thousands of recipes helps. When Peter and I cross California, we each travel ready to capture new sights. Sure enough, here they come.

Sometimes we'll drive together: Companionship is not just pleasant; there are times when it's essential. Often, stopping by a field, Peter will step out with camera in hand, while I rustle in a camera bag, snag a few extra shots, and often end up in conversation with a field hand driving by wondering who we are. Inevitably, those conversations are in Spanish, and part of my duty is to earn Peter enough time to photograph without interruption and to pose questions we'd accumulated that my interlocutor might be able to answer. As it happens, fluent Spanish is a field skill of mine, but it's of a long-practiced Castilian variant acquired over thirty years of research in Spain that invariably produces perplexity in field-side discussions—who IS this fey-sounding guy, speaking with an Andalusian lisp, but the size of man-mountain and effortlessly wielding jokes with the grave accent of a Conquistador? With time I explain, ask questions, and revel in the experience. Peter and I reunite, finish the conversation, and head to the next dairy, the next field crop, the next farm, a previously unseen variety or festival or taste. This is a voyage of many stops, many crops, many themes—and exposure to a goodly number of California dreams.

VISUALIZING AGRICULTURE

PETER GOIN

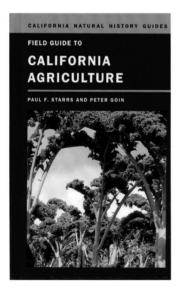

Who hasn't had the experience of driving by an agricultural field, looking out, and asking, "What IS that?" And so, yearning for answers to simple questions, Paul Starrs, my coauthor on the *Field Guide to California Agriculture*, and I began our journey more than a decade ago.

And what a journey it was. Perhaps there's no better way to start than to just jump in, and that's what we did, at the 2006 World Ag Expo. Tulare, California, home of the Expo, is in the heart of the San Joaquin Valley and at the center of California agriculture. Woven within California history, Tulare was named after the lake with the namesake tule (technically, a rush plant) lining the marshes and sloughs along the shoreline. The Yokuts people preceded Eurocentric and Mexican settlement, but their hold on the land dissipated with the onslaught of economic development. Tulare was incorporated in 1872, and then, not as an agricultural locus but as a headquarters for the Southern Pacific Railroad. By 1891 the railroad had moved its offices to Bakersfield, and the citizens of Tulare focused on agriculture by establishing

the Tulare Irrigation District. The rest, as the phrase goes, is history, but, in fact, history is continually written and rewritten.

Tulare burned down and was rebuilt three times in the fourteen years since its founding. In 1912, Hulett C. Merritt founded the (Tulare) Tagus Ranch, soon the largest fruit ranch in the world, and during WWII, portions of the Ranch served as a German prisoner of war camp. During the hysteria surrounding the Japanese bombing of Pearl Harbor in 1941, the U.S. Army took control of the Tulare County Fairgrounds establishing a detention center for Japanese Americans. This lasted just a little bit more than four months, until internees were moved to more permanent War Relocation Camps.

Today, the Tulare County Fairgrounds house the International Agri-Center, home to the World Ag Expo and the California Antique Farm Equipment Show. On a warm February California day, we entered the fairgrounds, instantly confronted with acre upon acre of green tractors, earth-mover tourist wagons, red tractors, decorated dairy cow statues, antique irrigation pump-fountains, blue tractors, Gophinators, cowhides on racks, trimmers, tillers, and dump trucks. And more upon more, naturally... a feast of agricultural innovation and mechanization, an industrial harbinger for solving every problem by primary-colored machines. For the uninitiated, half the time was spent trying to figure out what any specific machine actually was designed to do—without looking at the descriptions, of course. Hay balers were obvious but the tree trimmers looked suspiciously like some kind of Star Wars next-generation weapon, awaiting the appropriate white-suited storm troopers. Next aisle—white chemical suits, no doubt storm trooper underwear. Dairy Princesses may be slightly anachronistic, but smiling they were with sashes and tiaras. Giant harvesters abounded. We walked diligently, if flagging a bit, through rows and aisles of agricultural everything. We were stunningly overwhelmed. Next stop: black walnut groves.

There's no reason why black walnuts were next except that we had to start somewhere in the amazing grid of California agriculture. Usually, Paul drove his beloved Toyota Rav4, navigating us through back roads and byways while I did what photographers do best. That is, I look and see, yet become mesmerized by the perspective point of carefully planted line crops magically dissolving into an illusion of motion, flipping by alongside the roadway. What IS that, anyway? The motion denies measurement; it's an agricultural ocean of undulating waves of soybean and hay and orchards and row crops, galore.

Peaches, windfallen; acres and acres, overgrown. Gravenstein apples, no longer in vogue, left fermenting in Sebastapol groves. Water, water everywhere, but nary a drop to drink. Parched land, fruit laden trees; next, asparagus ferns, and homemade extruded aluminum irrigation siphons. Sunflowers everywhere waving silently for Van Gogh, birds asunder. Roma tomatoes piled into a mountain unto itself, good for canning or perhaps McDonalds. Turn the corner of an agriculturally efficient square-mile section, and a tattered paper sign announces a sale of organic heifers. That word *organic* mystifies us as it becomes a word with little meaning, at least so far as I can tell. Perhaps it's a feel-good word that means somebody cares about how the item was raised or grown. Or, perhaps it's just another word for *we're trying*. Alongside the drive, and it's always the drive, conversations take on a measuring tone with never a word to spare. There's a chaos of olives here and there, within a shallow depth of field, clusters abounding. Black-eyed peas are in my mind's eye as we sail in a slow-speed drive through under the Orland Arch. I started thinking—how many urban arches are there in California? We've been through lots. Orland, of course, Modesto's is the idealist's model, Burlingame, Castroville, Clovis, Fairfield, Fresno, Lodi, Pleasanton, Whittier, Williams, Willits, and no less, Weed and Yreka.

The naming of developed communities is always worth a thought or two. After all, the West is where we name streets after whatever it is that was vanquished. Trees, yes, or crops no longer grown; those apples, perhaps. Passing by Orangewood Estates with no oranges and no orchards but, soon, rice fields, rice, everywhere, a genial crop for humans or migrating birds on the Pacific Flyway. Butte County prunes and French plums, then onward through peaches and kiwi, pendulous. It's a delight and a cornucopia, as the trellis structures and irrigation pumps define the extended diverse landscapes. Honeydews are on display. Sudan grasses wave in the wind. Corn tassels tickle a blue sky. Barbed wire and chain link fences isolate long poultry sheds, without signage. A pink bollworm trap, noticed. Bees swarm. What is to become of the bees?

Driving, driving …we pass bundles of figs and then piles of grain, loading trucks and then, groves of pistachio trees. Pistachios date back to the Holy Lands of the Middle East, and were considered a rare delicacy. American traders imported the pistachio in the 1850s, and today, more than 98% of all pistachios grown in the United States are California-grown. Raisin grapes dangle under the sun, deep blue clusters rich in color. Thompson seedless grapes grow along Highway 145, south of Avenue 12 in Madera County …then the odd large orange-orange roadside stand. Nectarines and cucumbers and agricultural murals in Exeter, titled the "Golden Harvest." In Fresno County, a pile of sulfur contrasts with blue sky. Photographing a crop duster preparing for a test run, we were inundated with pink dye, everywhere: hats, shoes, camera bag. There must be something to the cliché of the flyboy crop duster. He flew that plane directly above us and unloaded. What *was* that stuff?

Driving back and forth, here and there, everywhere, alongside the tractor graveyard and then, later, passing by hooded, scarved workers pruning trellises with the Foster

Farms chicken processing plant in the distant horizon, reminiscent of the Wizard of Oz's great Kingdom. Sugar beets are another great agricultural story; flipping by, row upon row. Claus Spreckels was at first a railroad magnate but in 1896, he maneuvered Salinas growers to pledge 30,000 acres to grow sugar beets, enabling him to justify construction of a factory. Spreckels Sugar Co. was incorporated in August 1896 and expanded to eight plants that produced sugar until 1981. Since Salinas Valley was still undeveloped for farming, Spreckels purchased land for tenant farming, leasing each acre for $10 if the farmer grew sugar beets. He brought German laborers, hired Chinese and Japanese workers, and many ended up owning the land they farmed. And then, the Curly Top Virus brought on a blight creating swings in the prices of sugar as factories were forced to close. In part, this resulted in the founding of agriculture research departments and seed development programs within California universities. Innovation and adaption followed.

Chard, next, and then Star Route Farms in Bolinas, source for so much of the fare in fine Berkeley restaurants: think Alice Waters and Chez Panisse. Taking a break, we visit San Francisco's Ferry Plaza Farmer's Market, a cliché busman's holiday, but soon, and again, off to the roadways and byways of agricultural fields. The guide to everything fits with the Market—organic dried Haichya persimmons, radishes, Asian pears, horseradish leaves and root, purple potatoes and, well, beyond to snacks, antojitos, and fresh seafood, naturally. Check Chinese eggplant and Hog Island oysters off the list. I photographed the fresh oyster on the half-glove, reminiscent of *The Birth of Venus* (Sandro Botticelli, ca. 1485). Strawberry fields, forever…

The small Sacramento River towns are refuges from surrounding industrial fields, and engaging historical remnants provide evidence of the diversity of California agriculture's practitioners and inhabitants. Brannan Island, Isleton Joe's Restaurant & Saloon, Locke… creaking boardwalks harken to a lost era. We made the ferry crossing (free), at the junction of Cache Slough and the Sacramento River, heading to Ryer Island from north of Rio Vista, Solano County. Why? Because it was there. The diminution of the California oak woodland is ever on our minds. When ranch lands are converted to the lyrical *Live Oak Estates*, I wonder, too, about the majesty of the spreading oak and its abundance. The kaleidoscope of California agriculture gives little time to pause, as the next row crop, the next dairy, the next fruit stand, appears. Pumpkin patches are often the only "agricultural experience" that an urban dweller can normally have. Kale looks like broccoli, and do artichokes really grow like that? Or should I talk about how farm-to-table it is to have Brussels sprouts on a stem in Raley's grocery store, down the street. Stoop labor under the protection of a hoodie. Packing boxes and blue porta-potties, "how-much-does-this-pumpkin weigh" invoke an Agrilandia resort of fanciful delights, and I haven't even brought up mountains of compost, Kohlrabi, or purple cauliflower. Pink Ladies, prickly pear fruit, purple cabbage, and flowering broccoli add to the conundrum of complexity.

Photographing at the Johann Dairy near Fresno was hilarious as the dairy cows vie to be next in line to ride the carousel milking machine. In a large staging area, they jostle and edge each other, half-ton milk engines, entering the chute. Round they go in a full circle, only to be forced to back out by a cold-water spray directed at their face. Without the startling surprise, they wouldn't leave the comfort of reducing their milk load and riding the ride. Mechanized milking is new age scientific farming; hooked up, measured, tagged, and of course computerized. Cows and cats, silage and backhoes…all, together, in concert like a rural opera, except to say that all the singers are low mooers, with a couple of bellowers thrown in. The cat's presence was unexplained, except that cats are supposed to keep the cows content.

Paul and I traveled to the Annual Growers' Citrus Tasting Event conducted by the University of California, at the Lindcove Research and Extension Center, in December 2006. Walking into the room, the citrus smell boosted our body's production of serotonin, a hormone that makes you feel happy. This might be true or not, but we were content just to see so many experimental citrus varieties. There were Ceridwen Navel, Atwood Navel, and Leng Navel oranges. Limonette DeMar lemons, Vaniglia Sanguigno oranges, Yuzu, Mary Ellen sweet limes and Millsweet lemons, Cadenera sweet oranges, Thornless Mex limes, Flame grapefruit…Star Ruby grapefruit, pummelos, hybrid white grapefruits, and the spectacular Moro blood orange, Clementine Fina, a compromise between tangerine and pomerans (bitter orange). They were many more, and while I want to list them all, suffice it to say that the table itself reminded me of Leonardo da Vinci's *The Last Supper*. Crossing religions and metaphor mixing, there was of course the spectacular Buddha's Hand (Fingered Citron). The plethora of citrus made it another day at the circus.

Every orange is photographed eight times for size, character, flaws, shape…to clear those with any defect (photographed under black light), oranges are washed, conveyed, lined up, measured, and mechanically sorted into the appropriate divisions of premium, choice, juice, or cull. Some of the work is still overseen by hands wearing blue gloves. It's a fruit factory, to say nothing about the harvesting and the entire immigration debate, shades of fifty complexities. *La Migra* extends into the consciousness of every farm worker.

Paul and I traveled to the deserts, into Deglet Noor country, encountering many varieties of dates and palms. We saw *The Romance and Sex Life of the Date* in film and on display, and visited curio shops with tchotchkes made from every fruit design. Perhaps the avocado-serving dish would be a suitable present for a forthcoming holiday or birthday. Everybody should have one. They look authentic, if that matters.

Golf courses are defined as agricultural lands and their water allocation and utility is subsidized accordingly. The white balls are the fruits of leisure and are often found submerged awaiting a new form of rapture, or pollination. Just to be clear, there is a published *Golf Cookbook*. Next up, bok choy, for no particular reason except there it was, along the route. Continuing on the road, when we neared a dairy, Paul would inevitably say "ah, the smell of money" but what stands out for me is the smell of onions, preceding the visual. Garlic, sometimes, too, but onions permeate the air more noticeably if breathing deeply. Lettuce reminds us that water is wealth and the ostentatious display of water is a participle of California agriculture. Flood irrigation has to be seen to be believed, especially in Riverside County, averaging eleven inches of rainfall, annually. Water spinach, greenhouses, carrot foliage, and more lettuce fields. *The Lettuce Fields* could be the title of a novel; a mystery, perhaps, like the 1974 movie inspired by California water wars, *Chinatown*, starring Jack Nicholson and Faye Dunaway.

Let us not forget the cattle, scattered, but still in neat sociable groups. The irrigation canals are everywhere, too, crisscrossing the landscape like a Jeffersonian Grid suitable for an emerging American agri-technocracy. Channels, gates, pumping houses, and then, to punctuate a more layered inference, the *All-American Canal*. We drove by the Utopia Cattle Company sign, *Santa Gertrudis*. Pauma Valley and its rising casinos peppered within landscapes of avocados, citrus, and wildfire regions to the north, west, and east. We saw avocado trees reaching heights rarely seen in traditional orchards, heavy with fruit, fecund and frail. Reminiscing on my own youth living in Rio de Janeiro with a massive avocado tree in our front territory (not really a traditional yard, by any definition), I remember well what fresh avocado tastes like and wonder about how the packing and pre-ripe harvesting implies for what we taste in our stone fruit diet. Flavor is negotiated in favor of the vagaries of packing and time-to-table. My store-bought peaches more often rot rather than ripen, but this is probably more complicated than it sounds. I can't think about this much longer, as the kumquats sparkle in their yellow abundance against a bright sun. I'd never seen a Murcott blossom before. Now I have. Frost-damaged avocado trees harken climate change, but these are words made for fighting, apparently. Walking amongst the Valencia orange blossoms reminds me of a day when citrus lined the streets of suburban Los Angeles, and you could smell the sweet, tangy essence of life, itself.

Working in the fields is hard and many American citizens avoid this kind of labor. Throughout our fieldwork, we almost always encountered native speakers from Mexico and Central America, with only a few exceptions. My father worked summers picking lemons, although he didn't speak about it much. Near Stockton, I photographed laborers harvesting asparagus and that's bend-over-cut-and-grasp work, all day long. There are not many, if any, U-pick asparagus fields. Most of the communal harvesting operations are for sweet fruits, such as cherries or other berries, or apples, peaches, pears…stone fruits. The rules are important: You must buy what you pick, no climbing trees, no throwing fruit, no running, watch your kids, and no eating the fruit in the orchard. Seems fair to me, but it does attest to what can happen when urban dwellers experience agriculture infrequently. Throwing fruit is not very common amongst workers hired to harvest a crop. I can hardly imagine what would become of agriculture were that to happen.

Site of Propagation of the Thompson Seedless Grape, 2007, Peter Goin.

In 2016, there were 4,653 bonded wineries in California; 11,496 in the entirety of the United States. There might just as well be as many books and magazines about the wine industry, too. From Chardonnay Court to Pinot Drive to Zinfandel Lane in Napa Valley, from old growth vines to experimental aluminum grafted seals on Bordeaux varieties, the journey through California's industry of wine recontextualizes nature not as wilderness, but nature as agriculture. We toured the Armida Winery in Healdsburg, photographing the production of wine at its inception, from harvest to storage to fermentation. Armida's self-described wine mistress demonstrated each step, a personal tour. I still look for Armida's Pinot Noir at wine lists in restaurants. The words of wine making are common, perhaps, but therein is a story—crush, flow, drying, fermenting, storing, barrels, alcohol, sipping, tasting …at the end of October 2017, on a blackened hillside across the road from Napa Valley's signature vineyards, investigators have cordoned off driveways forming a protective seal around what is believed to be the origin of the most destructive and costly fire in California's history. These flames, wind-driven and ravenous, were catastrophic and shocking, scary and depressing.

Pastoral metaphors punctuate agricultural landscapes. More often they function as romantic elements within emerging subdivisions, such as Valley Glen in Solano County. At the Valley Glen gate, sculpted sheep and silent miniature windmills accentuate the view. Driving, driving, only to see plumes of smoke rise in the distant horizon as the Jepson Prairie Preserve burns. Partiers probably started the fire inadvertently by not fully extinguishing a late-night campfire. But in the Prairie, the winds were merciless. The Solano Land Trust in collaboration with the University of California Natural Reserve System manages the Jepson Prairie Preserve, one of the last remaining vernal pool and grassland habitats. While the fast moving fire burned to the horizon, locals were using the Preserve's hoses to try and extinguish the glowing embers left behind. Unfortunately, the role of fire has evolved beyond slash and burn into a new form of climate cataclysm.

Our journey continues, from the boutique pastures of devout Locavores replete with herds of goats to Berkeley's Monterey Market (pages 72 and 129), to safflower fields in bloom near Walker Landing along the Sacramento River. Pears, a holiday treat every winter, hang plump each with an emerging blush, heavy on branches, thick in clusters. Alfalfa flowers among the colors of California agriculture are rich, purple-blue, awaiting agri-nature's next step in the maturing process.

HISTORICAL MARKER

The role of cannabis in California agriculture is emerging from the shadows of an underground economy. Within the *Field Guide to California Agriculture*, we reported that cannabis cultivation was an industry estimated in value ranging from $19 billion to perhaps in excess of $40 billion—either number or anywhere in-between signifies a dominant force in California's agricultural industry. Photographing cannabis is an experience beyond any numbers—whether approved as a medical crop with suitable licensing, or as a function within the underground economy—at the time I was making photographs, I wondered about the legality of documenting an illegal crop. This could be guilt by association. The legalization of cannabis in California effective January 1, 2018, was something we could hardly have imagined when we wrote the *Field Guide*. The agricultural landscape is changing in unpredictable ways.

Hiding en route, taking back roads and backtracking, and going up and down un-named dirt roads festooned with *No Trespassing* signs into the darkening understory of coastal redwoods, a field emerged, green, rich, dark, dense. The plant itself is distinctive and odorous. My guide harvested and tended to the cannabis plants while I photographed; his hands were sticky and through some form of osmosis he was already enjoying the products of his labor. Needless to say, the plants responded well to his manicuring. Any one plant could be worth thousands in the underground economy—the sheer value of a single plant is nothing short of amazing.

The fieldwork for the *Guide* occupied more than seven years of traveling the agricultural byways of California. From the amazing mechanically trimmed apricot trees in San Joaquin County to the effervescent whiteness of cotton west of Los Banos, to co-op gins and fallow fields subsidized by the federal government *not to grow*, the journey was a slide down the tip of the discovery triangle. Into the landscapes of egrets, herons, hawks, and livestock, the fields are alive with the sounds of….everything agriculture. Remnants abound, either sweet potatoes or apples, abandoned packing crates or technostalgic farm equipment marketed in large roadside produce markets. Covered bell peppers and fields of flowers, cilantro, and nursery palm trees, roadside relics and suburban llama ranches, rooster sanctuaries and new developments in what-used-to-be cornfields have become the complexity of California Agriculture. When all is said and done, let us remember the workers, too. Let us remember those who toil in the landscape bringing food to table, literally, for the rest of us and for those, too, in far away lands. Remember the food trucks and the porta-potties, the minimalist housing and tent camps, the Quinceañeras and the parades, the Artichoke Festival, the Garlic Festival, the Carrot Festival, Indio Date Festival, and even, the Squirrel Roundup in Carlsbad.

When all is truly said and done, at least for one lifetime, may we all have "Water, Wealth, Contentment, Health."

When we started our multi-year journey, our premise was, and remains simple: As a rule, the generally urban population no longer knows much about agriculture, which is the predominant use of California's private land (and, given ranching, no insignificant part of its public land). Where does the food we eat come from? Who grows the crops? Who raises the animals? No, milk does not originate in the grocery store, but in a dairy, probably even a county or two distant. The *Field Guide to California Agriculture* reviews the roots of California agriculture and provides tools to understand farming, ranching, and the production of food, fuel, and fiber, then adds fitted lenses that help us grasp why and how California came to possess the most dramatic modern agricultural landscape in the world. The drama is physical and human, cultural and economic, sometimes heroic and at other times decidedly tragic. California agriculture is a compendium of delights, and stories.

A LAND OF PLENTY

From the Sierra Nevada to irrigated Mojave farmlands to the expansive Central Valley to cool, coastal ecoregions to the northern forests, California's varied ecosystems allow for agricultural production on a massive scale. The state produces 450+ commodities, accounting for more than a third of the country's vegetables and two-thirds of the country's fruits and nuts. Milk and cream, grapes, almonds, cattle and calves, lettuce, strawberries, pistachios, tomatoes, walnuts, and broilers comprise the top-ten valued commodities, and this doesn't even include the most probable number one crop, cannabis, generating in more recent estimates upwards of $25 billion annually. In Locavore parlance, California is not only a leader of the "farm-to-table" movement, it's also a leader in agricultural production *under-the-table*.

ARTIFACTS OF CALIFORNIA AGRICULTURE

Photography is an essential ingredient in telling the history of California's agricultural identity. Images of agriculture emerged from the earliest days of the history of photography. Shaping, promoting, and documenting agricultural diversity began instantaneously once an image could be chemically fixed onto a surface and saved for later viewing. Photography's role in elaborating agricultural history ramped up in the middle of the nineteenth century as early operators (as photographers were initially called) made series of views for the public's visual consumption. From daguerreotypes of distinguished captains of industry and their families to mammoth plate photographs of landscapes celebrating the pastoral and agricultural ideal, photography as a medium offered the means and potential not only to record slices of time, but to interpret, romanticize, and engage in the critical dialogue of the day through multifaceted cultural lenses.

During the 1860s and well into the next century, stereoscopes—or stereograms; a pair of images often mounted on a card creating the illusion of three-dimensionality when viewed through a stereoscope—were mass produced due to public demand. Agricultural themes were natural subjects, especially images of the spectacle of agriculture, from the biggest to the most dramatic to the most unusual. As early as 1857, the California State Agricultural Society hosted fairs that included competitions for photographers. Once photography became popularized as mass media, the recording of history forever changed. Daguerreotypes, waxed calotype negatives, salted paper prints, wet collodion negatives, albumen prints, carbon prints, and photogravures all contributed to the remarkable variety of nineteenth century photography. Each technique had its particular aesthetic and technical ingenuity that contributes to the magical and transformative study of light, entirely ripe for documentarians. All aspects of human life became suitable subjects for visual remembrance; the camera became, essentially, a mirror with a memory.

The rise of vernacular photography—that of the common, everyday variety—offers yet another glimpse through the first-person view often neglected in traditional historical accounts. Many thousands of photographs, snapshots, and family photograph albums made by amateur photographers over the past 160 years provide researchers with a wide-ranging view of daily events, family life, and leisure activities. With these resources at our disposal, the tale of California's agricultural empire is ready to be harvested, in words and in pictures.

While media such as drawing, woodblock printing, half-tone publishing, and painting have existed alongside and in many ways integrated with photographic history, what is reflected in the photographic image is the warp and weft of a complex weave; a fabric of the *real*. The essence of photography contains a fundamental connection to the reality of the view—of *what is*. Of course, *what is* implies a declarative view, an artifact of a moment in time, stated. Upon further investigation, what is *real* involves more than what is visible; the photograph by its very nature is layered in complexity, signs, and signifiers. Concurrent with the image of a slice in time, the photograph's meaning is deeply dependent upon the context of its viewing. If the transmission of visual information—photography, cartography, media-graphics including posters, advertisements, labels, and the vast amount of data reporting—is circumstantially a paradox both overt and discrete (and often the two are disconnected), the digital age is integrating these facets into a conglomerate of a newly-emerging chaotic visual-data culture. Only among the *illiterati* is photography merely illustrative rather than intrinsically valued as primary information, artifact, and historical document.

The view through an agricultural lens reveals a vantage point that is arguably unique, distinct by compositional structure and framing. The record of California agricultural photography invokes a fundamental aesthetic confounded by the sheer scale of agri-production. The diversity and polemics of production from labor relations to agribusiness economics influences and partially defines the context of how a photograph is viewed and interpreted. The visual narrative often emphasizes the structure of power—whether a corporate farm or a powerful agency—but what's amazing is that these images are ultimately dependent upon the context of their viewing. Viewers often re-contextualize a pictured scene through their own pre-determined cultural rubric. The photograph is malleable within a specifically defined contextual parameter, and alterable once that context changes. Ironically, what ensures a photograph's value is in part a function of consistent re-interpretation. This is a process that renders the images important, as they, through that continual reexamination, contribute to an ongoing meta-historical revisionism.

THE BANCROFT LIBRARY: PRESERVING CALIFORNIA'S AGRICULTURAL PAST

The visual history of California agriculture is hardly linear or chronological, as images, artwork, and commercial illustrations emerge from the dark depths of attics, storerooms, basements, or storage units long neglected. Firms devoted to an industrial-scale production of picture postcards or tourist-destined photographs, and manufacturers of crate labels or equipment advertisements generate archives of such size and scope that accessioning and cataloguing can be a formidable task for a library. The repositories of news organizations are now added to the public record, but, often, access is limited or the costs of reproduction are deemed exorbitant, taxing a researcher's budget and adding a sizable acquisition burden. What is lost, or denied due to institutional barriers, or leads an image to dissolve because of the vagaries of decay and time (especially with color film), denies our sense of ourselves, as history is relegated

to the remaining images that are publicly available, digitally scanned, usable, and (mostly) free. Archives are soulful repositories of place history. The means of images' survival are neither obvious nor guaranteed. Images are lost, either through casual disregard for the intrinsic value of the image itself, or lost through catastrophe, as with the San Francisco Earthquake fires in 1906. It takes a dedicated curator, such as Jack von Euw of the Bancroft Library, to make it his life's work to preserve the wonderful photographs of California and the evolving American West, and in this case, laud and acquire a compendium of photographs of California agriculture. It is important to recognize that many images and collections of someone's life work survived simply because somebody made the effort to save them. The debate over the authority of the historical narrative may never be fully resolved, but whatever is said and done, these artifacts provide a dramatic alternative to deeply structured historical narratives. Archives such as The Bancroft Library are essential to a civilized society, where ideas are valued and the visual artifacts of the least protected can be preserved. Hidden histories are resurrected as lost collections of photography are discovered and preserved within the public trust. And photographs become significant and telling artifacts, regardless of the original intent of their makers.

THE WISDOM OF AGRICULTURE

Our passion for photography lies within its hidden truths. In August 2007, a year and a half after that first introduction to the World Ag Expo, I noticed one of those signs that symbolizes the layered complexity of California agriculture while I was driving through agricultural lands on Highway 99 near Dairyville. Not that this one sign, or one image, reduces the entirety of agriculture to one message or product, but that it embodies the spirit of inventiveness, imagination, dedication, and pride of California farmers.

Signs represent a fundamental truth about the agricultural story. This sign references the pride of agriculture, the can-do spirit of farmers and ranchers, the tenacity of the agricultural enterprise, the visual richness of a fecund tomato, and the simple beauty of *what is real*. Photographing California agriculture means ingesting the signs and metaphors of perfunctory objectness—the crop is lettuce, or berries, or pistachios, or olives or everything grown or raised, there in full *color, like a ripe tomato*.

Yet the sub-culture of meaning resides in the references to a sense of place and art history. On another side of the faceted jewel of California's agriculture are the disguised workers toiling under a hoodie with rake, earning field-hand wages while ensuring timely harvesting that is critically important to growers and consumers. The countless workers come and they go, some stay, and where they live is even less known. Dorothea Lange's photographs are iconic reminders that there's a human element in the story of agriculture. The story is not just about the Dust Bowl, or intra-state migration, but desiring a better life, a healthier life, and not just for the consumers of agricultural commodities, but also for the workers in the fields, themselves.

As I photographed the sign, the lyrics of a Guy Clark song came to mind. *Home Grown Tomatoes* was recorded on Clark's fifth studio album *Better Days*.

Ain't nothing' in the world that I like better
Than bacon and lettuce and homegrown tomatoes
Up in the morning' out in the garden

Get you a ripe one don't get a hard one
Plant 'em in the spring eat 'em in the summer
All winter without 'em's a culinary bummer
I forget all about the sweatin' and digging'
Everytime I go out and pick me a big one

Homegrown tomatoes, homegrown tomatoes
What'd life be without homegrown tomatoes?
Only two things that money can't buy
That's true love and homegrown tomatoes

You can go out to eat and that's for sure
But it's nothing' a homegrown tomato won't cure
Put 'em in a salad, put 'em in a stew
You can make your very own tomato juice
Eat 'em with eggs, eat 'em with gravy
Eat 'em with beans, pinto or navy
Put 'em on the side put 'em in the middle
Put a homegrown tomato on a hotcake griddle

If I's to change this life I lead
I'd be Johnny Tomato Seed
'Cause I know what this country needs
Homegrown tomatoes in every yard you see
When I die don't bury me
In a box in a cemetery
Out in the garden would be much better
I could be pushin' up homegrown tomatoes

I thought to myself at the time that this was indeed an esoteric
reference and it's probable that even the maker of the sign
didn't realize the connection to the Guy Clark lyrics. The song
is really a tribute to the quiet side of life, the simple pleasures,
and the things that we do to enjoy the tranquility of a life in
the grand garden. The song romanticizes the bucolic lifestyle,
certainly, but it is true that money can't buy true love or
homegrown tomatoes. At the end of the day when the sun dips
below the horizon and the work's done, we can head home to
the dinner table knowing that there's wisdom in agriculture.

Home Grown Tomatoes, 2007, Peter Goin.

BANC DIG 2017.14:Ag00979

SOURCES AND SUGGESTED READINGS

Adams, Ansel, and Nancy Newhall. 1967. *Fiat Lux: The University of California*. New York: McGraw-Hill.

Alagona, Peter S., Antonio Linares, Pablo Campos, and Lynn Huntsinger. 2013. History and Recent Trends, In: *Mediterranean Oak Woodland Working Landscapes: Dehesas of Spain and Ranchlands of California*, edited by Pablo Campos, Lynn Huntsinger, José Oviedo, Paul F. Starrs, Mario Díaz, Richard B. Standiford, and Gregorio Montero, 25–58. Dordrecht: Springer.

Alagona, Peter S. 2013. *After the Grizzly: Endangered Species and the Politics of Place in California*. Berkeley: University of California Press.

Alexander, Kurtis. 2018. California Announces Tentative Funding for New Giant Dams. *San Francisco Chronicle*, 20 April. On-line at: www.sfchronicle.com/news /article/California-announces-tentative-funding-for-new-12851731. php?t=9fac14e8cc

Anderson, M. Kat. 2006. *Tending the Wild: Native American Knowledge and the Management of California's Natural Resources*. Berkeley: University of California Press.

Arax, Mark. 2011. *West of the West: Dreamers, Believers, Builders, and Killers in the Golden State*. New York: PublicAffairs.

Arax, Mark, and Rick Wartzman. 2003. *The King of California: J. G. Boswell and the Making of a Secret American Empire*. New York: PublicAffairs.

Arax, Mark, Trent Davis Bailey (photographs), and Denise Nestor (illustrations). 2018. A Kingdom from Dust. *The California Sunday Magazine*. 31 January. On-line at: story.californiasunday.com/resnick-a-kingdom-from-dust

Bailey, Liberty Hyde. 1905–06. What A University Farm is For, *The University Chronicle: An Official Record*, 8:49-54.

Balkin, Amy, Kim Stringfellow, and Tim Halbur. 2008. *Invisible-5 Audio Project*. Greenaction for Health and Environmental Justice, and Pond: Art, Activism, and Ideas; revised and updated in 2008. On-line at: invisible5.org/index. php?page=home

Bancroft, Hubert Howe. 2013. *Literary Industries: An Abridged Edition*, ed. Kim Bancroft Berkeley, California: Heyday Books.

Berry, Wendell. 1990. The Pleasures of Eating. In: *What Are People For? Essays by Wendell Berry*, 145–152. San Francisco: North Point Press.

Bittman, Mark. 2015. The Changing Faces of California Agriculture, 30 September, number three of a ten video series, *California Matters*, produced by *The New York Times* in collaboration with University of California Global Food Initiative. On-line at: www.youtube.com/watch?v=EHZvDR9oUFg and entire series is accessible at Mark Bittman Channel: On-line at: www.youtube.com/channel /UCl-FXGBB36Yd4xOFWSKc0Dg?sub_confirmation=1

Bonné, Jon. 2013. *The New California Wine: A Guide to the Producers and Wines Behind a Revolution in Taste*. Berkeley, CA: Ten Speed Press.

Booker, Matthew Morse. 2013. *Down by the Bay: San Francisco's History Between the Tides*. Berkeley and Los Angeles: University of California Press.

Broek, Jan O.M. 1932. *The Santa Clara Valley, California: A Study in Landscape Changes*. Utrecht: Uitgevers, Publicaties uit het Geographisch en uit het Mineralogisch instituut der Rijksuniversiteit te Utrecht.

Burcham, Levi T. (Lee). 1982. *California Range Land: An Historico-Ecological Study of the Range Resources of California*. Rev of 1957 edition, Publication Number 7. Davis, CA: Center for Archeological Research.

Burgess, Anika. 2018. How Photographers Captured the Incarceration of Japanese Americans during WWII. *Atlas Obscura*, 26 January. On-line at: www. atlasobscura.com/articles/how-photographer-captured-incarceration-japanese- americans-wwii-miyatake-lange-adams-albers

California Department of Food and Agriculture. 2017. *California Agricultural Statistics Review, 2015–2016*. Sacramento: State of California. On-line at: www.cdfa. ca.gov/statistics/PDFs/2016Report.pdf

Chan, Sucheng. 1986. *This Bittersweet Soil: The Chinese in California Agriculture, 1860–1910*. Berkeley: University of California Press.

_____. 1991. *Entry Denied: Exclusion and the Chinese Community in America, 1882–1943*. Philadelphia, PA: Temple University Press.

Clark, Guy. 1983. Home Grown Tomatoes from *Better Days* album, © Sony/ATV Music Publishing LLC. Also available at: On-line at: www.youtube.com/watch?v=1-QzLljL1u4

Cleland, Robert Glass. 1941. *Cattle on a Thousand Hills: Southern California, 1850–1880*. San Marino, CA: The Huntington Library.

Cole, Peter, David Struthers, and Kenyon Zimmer (eds.). 2017. *Wobblies of the World: A Global History of the IWW*. Chicago: University of Chicago Press.

Cross, Ira B. 1935. *A History of the Labor Movement in California*. Berkeley: University of California Press.

Cunningham, Laura. 2011. *A State of Change: Forgotten Landscapes of California*. Berkeley, CA: Heyday Books.

Daniel, Cletus E. 1981. *Bitter Harvest: A History of California Farmworkers, 1870–1941*. Ithaca, NY: Cornell University Press.

Daniels, Roger. 1962. *The Politics of Prejudice: The Anti-Japanese Movement in California and the Struggle for Japanese Exclusion*. Berkeley: University of California Press.

Dent, Borden. 1966. Irrigation Pumping and Pump Manufacturing in California. Master's thesis, Geography, UC Berkeley.

Didion, Joan. 1968. *Slouching towards Bethlehem*. New York: Farrar, Straus and Giroux.

Dominguez, Roseanne. 1992. The Decline of Santa Clara County's Fruit and Vegetable Canning Industry (1967–1987). Master's thesis, San José State University.

Doughty, Robin. 1975. *Feather Fashions and Bird Preservation: A Study in Nature Protection*. Berkeley and Los Angeles: University of California Press.

Elings, Mary W. (compiler). 2004. Finding Aid to the Maps of Private Land Grant Cases of California, 1840–1892. BANC Land Case Maps, The Bancroft Library. On-line at: pdf.oac.cdlib.org/pdf/berkeley/bancroft/mlandcasemap.pdf

Evetts, Rosemary, and Elizabeth Stephens (compilers). 1992. Finding Aid to the Miller & Lux Records, 1869–1965, revised 2006 and 2009; BANC MSS C–G 163, The Bancroft Library, On-line at: pdf.oac.cdlib.org/pdf/berkeley/bancroft/mcg163_cubanc.pdf

Fairfax, Sally K., Louise Nelson Dyble, Greig Tor Guthey, Lauren Gwin, Monica Moore, and Jennifer Sokolove. 2012. *California Cuisine and Just Food*. Boston, MA: The MIT Press.

Farmer, Jared. 2013. *Trees in Paradise: A California History*. New York: W.W. Norton.

Fullilove, Courtney. 2017. *The Profit of the Earth: The Global Seeds of American Agriculture*. Chicago: University of Chicago Press.

Galarza, Ernesto. 1964. *Merchants of Labor: The Mexican Bracero Story*. Charlotte, NC: McNally & Loftin.

Goin, Peter. 1996. *Humanature*. Austin: University of Texas Press.

Goldschmidt, Walter R. 1947. *As You Sow: Three Studies in the Social Consequences of Agribusiness*. Montclair, NJ: Allanheld, Osmun & Co. Publishers.

Gordon, Linda. 2006. Dorothea Lange: The Photographer as Agricultural Sociologist. *The Journal of American History*. 93(3):698–727.

Grahm, Randall. 2010. *Been Doon So Long: A Randall Grahm Vinthology*. Berkeley: University of California Press.

Gregory, James N. 1991. *American Exodus: The Dust Bowl Migration and Okie Culture in California*. New York: Oxford University Press.

Griffin, Paul F., and Ronald L. Chatham. 1958. Urban Impact on Agriculture in Santa Clara County, California. *Annals of the Association of American Geographers, 48*(3):195–208.

Grossinger, Robin M., Ruth A. Askevold, Charles J. Striplen, E. Brewster, S. Pearce, K. Cayce, L.J. McKee, and J.N. Collins. 2006. *Coyote Creek Watershed Historical Ecology Study: Historical Conditions and Landscape Change in the Eastern Santa Clara Valley, California*. SFEI Contribution No. 426, Richmond, CA: San Francisco Estuary Institute. On-line at: www.sfei.org/documents/coyote-creek-watershed-historical-ecology-study-historical-conditions-and-landscape-change

Grossinger, Robin M., and Ruth A. Askevold. 2012. *Napa Valley Historical Ecology Atlas: Exploring a Hidden Landscape of Transformation and Resilience*. Berkeley: University of California Press.

Guthman, Julie. 2004. *Agrarian Dreams: The Paradox of Organic Farming in California*. Berkeley and Los Angeles: University of California Press.

Gutiérrez, Ramón A., and Richard J. Orsi (eds.). 1998. *Contested Eden: California before the Gold Rush*. Berkeley and Los Angeles: University of California Press, with the California Historical Society.

Hanson, Victor Davis. 1999. *The Other Greeks: The Family Farm and the Agrarian Roots of Western Civilization*. 2nd ed. Berkeley: University of California Press.

Harkinson, Josh. 2013. How Industrial Pot Growers Ravage the Land: A Google Earth Tour. *Mother Jones,* 06 February. On-line at: www.motherjones.com/food/2013/02/google-earth-tour-marijuana-farms-environment-video/#

Hart, John Fraser. 1991. The Perimetropolitan Bow Wave. *Geographical Review 81*(1): 35–51.

Haslam, Gerald W. 1994. *The Other California: The Great Central Valley in Life and Letters,* rev. and enlarged. Reno and Las Vegas: University of Nevada Press.

Hirschmann, Jan V. 2007. The Early History of Coccidiomycosis: 1892–1945. *Clinical Infectious Diseases, 44*:1202–1207.

Holley, Peter, and Christie Hemm Klok. 2018. The Silicon Valley Elite's Latest Status Symbol: Chickens. *The Washington Post,* 2 March. On-line at: www.washingtonpost.com/news/business/wp/2018/03/02/feature/the-silicon-valley-elites-latest-status-symbol-chickens/?utm_term=.6abcab18c58f

Hundley, Norris, Jr. 2001. *The Great Thirst: Californians and Water: A History*, rev. ed. Berkeley and Los Angeles: University of California Press.

Igler, David. 2001. *Industrial Cowboys: Miller & Lux and the Transformation of the Far West, 1850–1929.* Berkeley and Los Angeles: University of California Press.

Isenberg, Andrew C. 2005. *Mining California: An Ecological History.* New York: Hill and Wang, a division of Farrar, Straus, and Giroux.

Ivey, Linda L. 2007. Ethnicity in the Land: Lost Stories in California Agriculture. *Agricultural History, 81*(1):98–124.

Jacobson, Yvonne. 1984. *Passing Farms: Enduring Values—California's Santa Clara Valley.* Los Altos, CA: William Kaufmann, Inc.

Johnson, Stephen, Gerald Haslam, and Robert Dawson. 1993. *The Great Central Valley: California's Heartland.* Berkeley and Los Angeles: University of California Press, in Association with the California Academy of Sciences.

Jordan, Miriam, and Jennifer Medina. 2018. 'I am a Pawn': Trump's Immigration Fight with California Squeezes Those Caught in the Middle. *New York Times Magazine,* 08 March, On-line at: www.nytimes.com/2018/03/08/us/immigration-california-trump-sessions.html

Kahrl, William L., and William A. Bowen (eds.) 1979. *The California Water Atlas,* with Marlyn L. Shelton. Sacramento: State of California

Kahrl, William L. 1982. *Water and Power: The Conflict over Los Angeles' Water Supply in the Owens Valley.* Berkeley and Los Angeles: University of California Press.

Kelley, Robert L. 1959. *Gold vs. Grain: The Hydraulic Mining Controversy in California's Sacramento Valley; A Chapter in the Decline of the Concept of Laissez Faire.* Glendale, CA: The Arthur H. Clark Company.

_____. 1989. *Battling the Inland Sea: American Political Culture, Public Policy, and the Sacramento Valley, 1850–1986.* Berkeley and Los Angeles: University of California Press.

Kerr, Clark, E.T. Grether, and Harry R. Wellman. 1985. Paul Schuster Taylor [1895–1984, Professor Emeritus], Economics: Berkeley. *In Memoriam,* On-line at: texts.cdlib.org/view?docId=hb4d5nb20m&doc.view=frames&chunk.id=div00161&toc.depth=1&toc.id=

Kingsolver, Barbara, Camille Kingsolver, and Steven L. Hopp. 2007. *Animal, Vegetable, Miracle: A Year of Food Life.* New York: Harper.

Leopold, A. Starker, and Tupper Ansel Blake. 1985. *Wild California: Vanishing Lands, Vanishing Wildlife.* Berkeley and Los Angeles: University of California Press.

Liebman, Ellen. 1983. *California Farmland: A History of Large Agricultural Land Holdings.* Totowa, N.J.: Rowman & Allanheld.

Lillard, Richard G. 1966. *Eden in Jeopardy: Man's Prodigal Meddling with His Environment.* New York: Alfred A. Knopf.

Loewe, Emma. 2018. A Look Inside the California Water Crisis that Nobody's Talking About, *MBG Planet,* 20 April. On-line at: www.mindbodygreen.com/articles/the-water-access-crisis-in-california

Malone, Michael S. 2002. *The Valley of Heart's Delight: A Silicon Valley Notebook, 1963–2001.* New York: John Wiley & Sons.

McClelland, Gordon T., and Jay T. Last. 1985. *California Orange Box Labels.* Beverly Hills, CA: Hillcrest Press.

MacCurdy, Rahno. 1925. *The History of the California Fruit Growers Exchange.* Los Angeles, CA: G. Rice and Sons.

McWilliams, Carey. 1942. *Factories in the Field: The Story of Migratory Farm Labor in California.* Boston, MA: Little, Brown and Co.

_____. 1973 [1946]. *Southern California: An Island on the Land.* Santa Barbara, CA, and Salt Lake City, UT: Peregrine Smith, Inc.

_____. 1976 [1949]. *California: The Great Exception.* Santa Barbara, CA, and Salt Lake City, UT: Peregrine Smith, Inc.

Masakazu, Iwata. 1962. The Japanese in California Agriculture. *Agricultural History* 36(1):25–37.

Masumoto, David Mas. 1996. *Epitaph for a Peach: Four Seasons on My Family Farm.* New York: HarperOne.

_____. 2009. *Wisdom of the Last Farmer: Harvesting Legacies from the Land.* New York: Free Press.

Matsumoto, Valerie. 1993. *Farming the Home Place: A Japanese American Community in California, 1919–1982.* Ithaca, NY: Cornell University Press.

Matthews, Glenna. 1985. The Apricot War: A Study of the Changing Fruit Industry During the 1930s. *Agricultural History,* 59(1):25–39.

May, Meredith, and Alice Walker. 2011. Fresh Eggs Hatch "Chicken Chronicles," [Interview with Alice Walker]: *San Francisco Chronicle,* 07 June. On-line at: www.sfgate.com/entertainment/article/Alice-Walker-Fresh-eggs-hatch-Chicken-2368228.php

Miller, M. Catherine. 1993. *Flooding the Courtrooms: Law and Water in the Far West.* Lincoln: University of Nebraska Press.

Mobley, Esther. 2018. Battle for Napa Valley's Future: Proposed Curb on Vineyards Divides County, *San Francisco Chronicle,* 08 April, updated 10 April. On-line at: www. sfchronicle.com/wine/article/The-battle-for-the-future-of-Napa-Valley -12816588.php

Mora, Jo. 1949. *Californios: The Saga of the Hard-Riding Vaqueros, America's First Cowboys.* Garden City, New York: Doubleday & Company, Inc.

Nabhan, Gary Paul. 2002. *Coming Home to Eat: The Pleasures and Politics of Local Foods.* New York: W. W. Norton & Company.

Naef, Weston, and Christine Hult-Lewis. 2011. *Carleton Watkins: The Complete Mammoth Photographs,* Los Angeles, CA: J. Paul Getty Museum.

Nickel, George Wilmarth, Jr., and Jamy Faulhaber (interviewer). 2002. Following the Cattle King: A Lifetime of Agriculture, Water Management, and Water Conservation in California's Central Valley. An oral History from interviews conducted with George W. Nickel, Jr., 1998–2001. Regional Oral History Office, University of California,Berkeley. On-line at: content.cdlib.org/view?docId=kt238nb0f4 &brand=calisphere&doc.view=entire_text

Ogden, Adele. 1929. Boston Hide Droghers along California Shores, *Quarterly of the California Historical Society [California Historical Society Quarterly]* 8(4): 289–305.

Palmquist, Peter E. 1983. *Carleton E. Watkins, Photographer of the American West.* Fort Worth, TX: Amon Carter Museum.

Palmquist, Peter E., and Thomas R. Kailbourn. 2002. *Pioneer Photographers of the Far West: A Biographical Dictionary, 1840–1865.* Stanford, CA: Stanford University Press.

Parker-Pope, Tara. 2018. When Is It Safe to Eat Salad Again? *The New York Times,* 19 April. On-line at: www.nytimes.com/2018/04/19/well/eat/romaine-lettuce -salad-food-poisoning-e-coli.html

Parsons, James J. 1940. Hops in Early California Agriculture. *Agricultural History* 14(3):110–116.

_____. 1986. A Geographer Looks at the San Joaquin Valley. *Geographical Review* 76(3):371–389.

Parsons, James J., and Paul F. Starrs. 1988. The San Joaquin Valley: Agricultural Cornucopia. *Focus* (American Geographical Society) 38(1):cover, 7–11.

Pollan, Michael. 2006. *The Omnivore's Dilemma: A Natural History of Four Meals.* New York, Penguin Press.

_____. 2008. *In Defense of Food: An Eater's Manifesto.* New York: Penguin.

Preston, William L. 1981. *Vanishing Landscapes: Land and Life in the Tulare Lake Basin.* Berkeley and Los Angeles: University of California Press.

_____. 1998. Serpent in the Garden: Environmental Change in Colonial California. In: *Contested Eden: California before the Gold Rush,* edited by Ramón Gutiérrez and Richard J. Orsi, 260–298. Berkeley and Los Angeles: University of California Press, with the California Historical Society.

Reisner, Marc. 1986. *Cadillac Desert: The American West and its Disappearing Water.* New York: Penguin Books.

Rorabaugh, William. 1989. *Berkeley at War: The 1960s.* New York: Oxford University Press.

Sackman, Douglas Cazaux. 2005. *Orange Empire: California and the Fruits of Eden.* Berkeley: University of California Press.

Sayre, Nathan F. 2017. *The Politics of Scale: A History of Rangeland Science.* Chicago: University of Chicago Press.

Scheuring, Ann Foley (ed.). 1983. *A Guidebook to California Agriculture by Faculty and Staff of the University of California.* Berkeley and Los Angeles: University of California Press.

Schnirring, Lisa. 2007. FDA Releases Final Report on Spinach E. coli Outbreak. *CIDRAP [Center for Infectious Disease Research and Policy],* 23 March. On-line at: cidrap.umn.edu/news-perspective/2007/03/fda-releases-final-report-spinach-e-coli-outbreak

Schoch, Deborah. 2011. Five Years after Deadly E. coli Outbreak, Salinas Valley Farmers Struggle to Rebound. *Mercury News* (San Jose, CA). 25 November. On-line at: www.mercurynews.com/2011/11/25/five-years-after-deadly-e-coli-outbreak-salinas-valley-farmers-struggle-to-rebound/

Smith, Charles Edward. 1940. Epidemiology of Acute Coccidiomycosis with Erythema Nodosum ("San Joaquin" or "Valley Fever"). *American Journal of Public Health* 30:600–611.

Smith, J. Russell. 1987 [1929]. *Tree Crops: A Permanent Agriculture,* reissued ed. Washington, D.C.: Island Press.

Spalding, William A. 1885. *The Orange: Its Culture in California.* Riverside, CA: Press and Horticulturist Steam Print.

Spirn, Anne W. 2008. *Daring to Look: Dorothea Lange's Photographs & Reports from the Field.* Chicago: University of Chicago Press.

Stanford, B., R.M. Grossinger, J. Beagle, R.A. Askevold, R.A. Leidy, E.E. Beller, M. Salomon, C.J. Striplin, and A. Whipple. 2013. *Alameda Creek Watershed Historical Ecology Study.* Richmond, CA: San Francisco Estuary Institute. On-line at: www.sfei.org/documents/alameda-creek-watershed-historical-ecology-study

Starr, Kevin. 1985. *Inventing the Dream: California through the Progressive Era.* New York: Oxford.

_____. 1990. *Material Dreams: Southern California through the 1920s.* New York: Oxford.

_____. 1997. *Endangered Dreams: The Great Depression in California.* New York: Oxford.

Starrs, Paul F. 1988. The Navel of California and Other Oranges: Images of California and the Orange Crate. *California Geographer* 27:1–42.

_____. 1998. *Let the Cowboy Ride: Cattle Ranching in the American West.* Baltimore, MD: Johns Hopkins University Press.

_____. 2007. Picturing California & the West: The 'Competent Vaquero,' Ed Borein, In: *Coloring the West: Watercolors and Oils by Edward Borein,* 5–23. Santa Barbara, CA: Santa Barbara Historical Museum.

Starrs, Paul F., and Lynn Huntsinger. 1998. The Cowboy & Buckaroo in American Ranch Hand Styles. *Rangelands* 20(5):36–40.

Starrs, Paul F., and Peter Goin. 2010. *A Field Guide to California Agriculture.* Berkeley and Los Angeles: University of California Press.

Stein, Walter J. 1973. *California and the Dust Bowl Migration.* Westport, CT: Greenwood Press, Inc.

Steinbeck, John. 1939. *The Grapes of Wrath.* New York: Viking Press.

_____. 1952. *East of Eden.* New York: Viking Press.

_____. 1995 [1938]. *The Long Valley.* New York: Penguin Books.

Stienstra, Tom. 2008. DFG's [Department of Fish and Game] Abalone Checkpoint Bags Pot Merchants. *San Francisco Chronicle,* 02 Nov. On-line at: www.sfgate.com/cgi-bin/article.cgi?f=/c/a/2008/11/02/SPTQ13QPD0.DTL&type=printable

Stine, Scott W. 1980. Hunting and the Faunal Landscape: Subsistence and Commerical Venery in Early California, Master's thesis, Geography, University of California at Berkeley.

Stoll, Steven. 1998. *The Fruits of Natural Advantage: Making the Industrial Countryside in California.* Berkeley: University of California Press.

Street, Richard Steven. 2004. *Photographing Farmworkers in California.* Stanford, CA: Stanford University Press.

Streshinsky, Ted (creator). Ted Streshinsky Photograph Archive, Box B. The Bancroft Library. On-line at: www.oac.cdlib.org/search?query=Ted%20Streshinsky%20;idT=UCb163084543

Taber, George. M. 2005. *Judgment of Paris: California vs. France and the Historic 1976 Paris Tasting That Revolutionized Wine.* New York: Scribner.

Takaki, Ronald T. 1984. *Pau Hana: Plantation Life and Labor in Hawaii, 1835–1920.* Honolulu: University of Hawaii Press.

Thwaites, Reuben G. 1905–06. Report on The Bancroft Library, *The University Chronicle: An Official Record,* 8:143.

Tsu, Cecilia. 2006. "Independent of the Unskilled Chinaman": Race, Labor, and Family Farming in California's Santa Clara Valley. *Western Historical Quarterly* 37(4):474–495.

Vaughn, Thomas. 1989. *Soft Gold: The Fur Trade & Cultural Exchange on the Northwest Coast of America.* Portland: Oregon Historical Society Press.

Vaught, David. 2007. *After the Gold Rush: Tarnished Dreams in the Sacramento Valley.* Baltimore, MD: The Johns Hopkins University Press.

Vink, Erik. 1998. Land Trusts Conserve California Farmland. *California Agriculture* 52(3):27–31.

Vischer, Edward. 1982. *Edward Vischer's Drawings of the California Missions, 1861–1878,* with a biography of the artist by Jeanne Van Nostrand. San Francisco: The Book Club of California.

von Euw, Jack, and Genoa Shepley. 2004. *Drawn West: Selections from the Robert B. Honeyman Jr. Collection of Early Californian and Western Art and Americana.* Berkeley, CA: Heyday Books and The Bancroft Library, University of California.

Walker, Alice. 2012. *The Chicken Chronicles: Sitting with the Angels Who Have Returned with My Memories: Glorious, Rufus, Gertrude Stein, Splendor, Hortensia, Agnes of God, the Gladyses, & Babe: A Memoir.* New York: The New Press.

Wallach, Bret. 1980. The West Side Oil Fields of California. *Geographical Review* 70(1):50–59.

Watt, Laura A. 2016. *The Paradox of Preservation: Wilderness and Working Landscapes at Point Reyes National Seashore.* Berkeley: University of California Press.

Wickson, Edward J. 1889. *The California Fruits and How to Grow Them: A Manual of Methods Which Have Yielded Greatest Success; With Lists of Varieties Best Adapted to the Different Districts of the State.* San Francisco, CA: Dewey & Co. and the Pacific Rural Press.

_____. 1917. *The California Vegetables in Garden and Field: A Manual of Practice with and without Irrigation for Semi-Tropical Countries.* San Francisco, CA: Pacific Rural Press.

Wilson, Bee. 2008. *Swindled: The Dark History of Food Fraud, from Poisoned Candy to Counterfeit Coffee.* Princeton, NJ: Princeton University Press.

Worster, Donald. 1982. Hydraulic Society in California: An Ecological Interpretation. *Agricultural History* 56(3):501–515.

Wyman, Mark. 2010. *Hoboes: Bindlestiffs, Fruit Tramps, and the Harvesting of the West.* New York: Hill & Wang.

Yogi, Stan (ed.). 1996. *Highway 99: A Literary Journey through California's Great Central Valley.* Berkeley, CA: Heyday Books, with the California Council for the Humanities.

MAJOR CALIFORNIA AGRICULTURE COLLECTIONS
AT THE BANCROFT LIBRARY

COLLECTIONS INCLUDED:

Call Number	Title	Extent
BANC PIC 1905.12780–.12821	Misc. California Views	42 prints
BANC PIC 1952.002—AX	Kern County Views from the Keith-McHenry Pond Collection	28 prints
BANC PIC 1973.056-PIC	Agriculture and flood-related photographs from Miller & Lux archive	110 prints / 1000 linear feet
BANC PIC 1983.098	Photographs relating to George Blowers	300 prints
BANC PIC 1983.224—ALB	Views of El Solyo Ranch, Vernalis Calif.	8 prints
BANC PIC 2008.050	Kings County Packing Co. photograph collection	42 prints
BANC PIC 2011.020—PIC	Charles B. Turrill photographs of San Francisco, Yosemite Valley, and other California locations	60 prints
BANC MSS 2002/192	Pleasants Family papers, 1859–1917	0.5 linear feet
BANC MSS 2010/192c	Otis H. Lockhart records: Los Angeles, 1898–1917	2.5 linear feet
BANC MSS 91/110c	Scrapbooks on the Dyer family and sugarbeet industry, 1850–1963	0.5 linear feet
BANC MSS 99/195c	W.R. Ralston papers relating to California agriculture, 1918–1949	2.5 linear feet
BANC MSS C-D 418	The Haraszthy family, San Francisco, manuscript, 1886	0.5 linear feet
BANC MSS C-G 163	Miller & Lux records, ca. 1869–1965	1,037 linear feet
BANC MSS P-D 16	William C. Land dictation, ca. 1888	0.25 linear feet
BANC CU-20	Records of the College of Agriculture, University of California, 1881–ongoing	43 linear feet
BANC PIC 1905.04663–.05242	Alice Iola Hare photograph collection	575 prints
BANC PIC 1988.103—STER	Views of the Buena Vista vineyards and winery, Sonoma County, Calif, by Eadweard Muybridge	18 prints
BANC PIC 1905.02634–.02731—PIC	Photographs of agricultural laborers in California by Ira B. Cross	97 prints
BANC PIC 1942.008	Farm Security Administration photograph collection	6 linear feet
BANC MSS 70/110c	Charles Frederick Fisk papers, 1863–1960	14 linear feet
BANC MSS 67/171c	Schmidt Lithograph Company records, ca. 1912–1929	20 linear feet
BANC PIC 1963. 002:0001–1886	Robert B. Honeyman Jr. collection of early Californian and Western American pictorial material	2,342 including dozens of framed items

BANC PIC 1979.034—ALB	Scenes from various San Francisco Bay Area Locations, ca. 1890s	50 prints
BANC PIC 1967.047—A	National Council on Agriculture Life and Labor Photographs	128 prints
BANC PIC 1979.084—.085	M.W. Talbot collection of forestry and agriculture photographs	1500 prints 285 slides and 39 lantern slides
BANC PIC 2012.089—fALB	N.H. Reed photograph album of Santa Barbara and vicinity	51 prints
BANC PIC 1959.085	California agriculture photographs collected or photographed by Frank Adams	103 prints, 440 lantern slides, 459 nitrate negatives
BANC PIC 19xx.054—PIC	Imperial Valley snapshots	23 prints
Land case map B-488	Plano del parage conscido por Rancho de Quito..	
BANC PIC 1941.004—ALB	Miscellaneous California and Mexico views	49 prints
BANC PIC 1905.06484—06485	Views from a trip to California, by Harriet S. Tolman	217 prints
BANC PIC 1974.019—ALB	Photographic views of El Verano and vicinity, Sonoma Valley, California, by Carleton E. Watkins	133 prints
BANC PIC 1905.06211—PIC	Riverside and Los Angeles area views	52 prints
BANC PIC 1977.019—ALB	Rivergarden Farms, photographed by McCurry Foto Co.	79 prints
BANC PIC 1954.013—PIC	Migrant labor camp photographs from the Harry Everett Drobish papers	63 prints
BANC PIC 2008.013	Central Valley, Calif. Farming photographs	14 prints
BANC PIC 2011.022	Peter Goin and Paul F. Starrs California Agriculture Archive, 2004—2013	notebooks, atlases, fieldwork guides 250 prints
BANC PIC 2013.047	Portfolio of Photographs of California Agriculture by Peter Goin	64 digital archival pigment prints in clamshell case
BANC DIG 2017.014	Peter Goin Digital Photograph Archive: The Colors of California Agriculture	approx. 1500 TIFs

BANC MSS 67/81c	Walter Eugene Packard family papers 1818–1973	
	(includes photographs transferred to Pictorial Collection)	25 linear feet
BANC MSS 73/140c	Hollister family papers: additions 1870–1973	1.3 linear feet
BANC MSS 69/57c	Hollister family papers 1874–1969	35.35 linear feet
BANC MSS 84/38	Paul Schuster Taylor papers 1960–1997	93 cartons, 22 boxes,
		2 oversize =106 ft
BANC MSS 87/20	David Weeks papers, 1912–1967	6.5 linear feet
BANC MSS C-R 18	J.N. Bowman papers, 1890–1965	9.5 linear feet
BANC MSS C-B967	John Samuel Watson papers, 1952–1962	3.2 linear feet
BANC MSS 2009/109	Murray R. Benedict papers, 1910–1984	32 linear feet
BANC MSS C-B 780	George P. Clements papers, 1920–1946	22 linear feet
BANC MSS C-R 1	Ralph W. Hollenberg collection of materials	
	relating to the Farm Security Administration,	
	Region IX, 1924–1949	11.25 linear feet
BANC MSS C-R 2	Federal Writer's Project source material on	
	Migratory Labor, District No. 8, c. 1936–1939	48 linear feet
BANC MSS 72/187c	Monographs prepared for a documentary	
	history of migratory farm labor, 1938	1 linear foot
BANC MSS C-G76	Russell B. Blowers and Sons records, 1887–1921	7 linear feet
BANC MSS 2004/120c	James Parker Diaries, 1891–1919	0.85 linear feet
BANC MSS C-G 181	American Seedless Raisin Company records,	
	1894–1956	17 linear feet
BANC MSS C-G 77	M. Theo Kearney papers, 1865–1906	2.9 linear feet
BANC MSS C-G 63	Kearney Ranch records, 1873–1949	35 linear feet
BANC MSS 2004/203c	Thomas C. Finney diaries, 1867–1872	1 linear foot
BANC MSS 70/110c	Charles Frederick Fisk papers, 1863–1960	14 linear feet
BANC MSS 78/57c	Cooper-Molera family papers, 1803–1970	9 linear feet
BANC MSS 69/16	Edward F. Adams collection, 1850–1958	2 linear feet
BANC MSS 68/97c	McCulloh family papers, 1852–1936	1.5 linear feet
BANC MSS 77/111c	Irving W. Wood papers, 1934–1937	0.5 linear feet
BANC MSS C-B 760	Charles Collin Teague papers, 1901–1950	55 linear feet
BANC MSS C-B 529	Harry Everett Drobish papers, 1917–1954	12 linear feet

ACKNOWLEDGEMENTS

Colors of California Agriculture is a collective undertaking, the result of efforts pulling toward a common cause and destination. Peter Goin and Paul F. Starrs worked with dozens of accomplished scholars, artists, and students to create *Colors of California Agriculture,* and offer thanks to all who have made this a better book.

Director Elaine Tennant and Jack von Euw at The Bancroft Library were steadfast in their enthusiasm for this book and made sure it happened—through thick and thin, including many a deliberative working lunch session that added distinctive contributions. Peter Hanff and Diana Vergil on The Bancroft Library staff were expert in navigating complicated issues of finance and book placement within the Keepsake series. Lorna Kirwan and Jennie Hutchings, in the duplication and photography division of Bancroft Public Services, made sure items that required scanning for the book would be available. An earlier Bancroft Gallery exhibition by the authors mid-year 2013 showcased less than 30% of the material included in this book, and as the "Major Collections" listing that precedes this makes clear, agriculture-related holdings at The Bancroft Library are broad, deep, and fascinating.

Jack von Euw offers particular thanks to Peter Goin for the generous gift of his extraordinary photographs; thanks Paul Starrs for his deep knowledge of California agriculture expressed in his colorful and accessible text; and recognizes the support of Bancroft Library Director emeritus Charles Faulhaber and Director Elaine Tennant for their roles in making the Colors of California Agriculture exhibition and Keepsake happen.

Christine Hult-Lewis at The Bancroft Library located wayward images, provided essential citation information, and made certain that the scans of Bancroft materials were complete and of acceptable quality, and as a scholar of photography, her expertise and enthusiasm was most welcome. At the University of Nevada, Elise Brodsky assisted with image preparation.

The Black Rock Institute Press handled production details for this book, and cooperation between The Bancroft Library and the Institute never flagged. At the Black Rock Institute, Donna Macknet kept accounts and numbers straight, and is, as always, a force for the good in a small nonprofit world that is in part keeping the book business and long-form scholarship and the visual arts alive. Kristin Selinder Mac-Donald handled copyediting and review of the manuscript text, and Dawn M. McCusker designed the book and handled compositing and production.

Colors of California Agriculture, conceived as a novel way to understand California's agricultural past and its innovative present-day, offers testimony to the generosity of spirit, hard work, and support from many who believe in the essential importance of agriculture for citizens of California—and, indeed, the world.

ABOUT THE AUTHORS

Peter Goin is Foundation Professor of Art in Photography and Time-based Media at the University of Nevada. Peter spent his formative years abroad, in Indonesia, Turkey, and Brazil, before returning to the United States to complete his education. After stretches living in Fairfax, Virginia; Washington, D.C.; and Oxford, Iowa, Peter moved to San Francisco, and ultimately to Nevada, where he lives today. Peter Goin produces photographs dealing with the long-term impact of culture and technology on the environment. Using the language of the Fine Arts, Peter's work integrates history, architecture, urban planning, and the social and political sciences in an interdisciplinary manner. He has authored or coauthored 20 books with such prestigious publishers as Johns Hopkins University Press, the University of California Press, the University of Texas Press, the Center for American Places, and Norton Publishers. Peter's work is included in more than 43 major collections ranging from the Whitney Museum of Art and the Museum of Modern Art in New York to the San Francisco Museum of Modern Art. The Library of Congress alone owns 350 of his photographs.

Peter's books include *Tracing the Line: A Photographic Survey of the Mexican-American Border*, *Nuclear Landscapes*, and *Stopping Time: A Rephotographic Survey of Lake Tahoe*. His *Humanature* explores and documents, through photography and text, the premise that nature is a cultural construct. *Changing Mines in America* reinterprets the legacy and importance of mining landscapes in the United States. Peter and Lucy Lippard coauthored the rephotographic survey *Time and Time Again: History, Rephotography, and Preservation in the Chaco World*. Peter's coauthored book *A New Form of Beauty: Glen Canyon Beyond Climate Change* explores new paradigms of the necessity for ruins. Working as the lead author with poet Gary Snyder, Peter was instrumental in the publication of *Dooby Lane*.

Peter's family includes longstanding Californians who began their permanent residence in California in 1919, although earlier ancestors arrived in Oregon by wagon train in 1853. Peter's father, during his time at UC Berkeley, worked as a seasonal farm worker in the lemon groves. Roots run deep.

Paul F. Starrs is on the faculty at the University of Nevada where he is the Regents & Foundation Distinguished Professor of Geography. A resident of both Nevada and California, Paul's journey to work across the Sierra has if nothing else taught him the turns and tarmac of every intriguing Sierra Nevada back road. Born in Bordeaux, France, the child of

U.S. diplomats, Paul spent much of the 14 years that followed in France, Spain, Guatemala, and Mexico. He is author of *Let the Cowboy Ride: Cattle Ranching in the American West* and, with Peter Goin, of *Black Rock*, an intimate look at a remote northwestern edge of Nevada, and a contributor to dozens of other books. Over the last ten years, Paul has written about film noir, Las Vegas, Santa Barbara artist Ed Borein, Mexican miners, rock art, the oak woodlands of Spain and Portugal, cowboy poetry and literature, Big Data, snow harvest, memoirs, John Brinckerhoff Jack-son, Mormon church architecture, the Ry Cooder CD *Chávez Ravine*, ranching and long-distance livestock trailing—the last in both worldwide and North American contexts.

A student through the late 1970s at Deep Springs College (California), Paul worked as a ranch hand in Nevada and eastern California when he concluded his time at Deep Springs, watching over several hundred cows and their calves grazing rangelands up to 13,100 feet elevation. After earning an honors undergraduate degree at UC San Diego researching intentional communities, postmodern poetry, and utopian thought, Paul continued his studies with a PhD in geography at the University of California, Berkeley. Through graduate school years and after, Paul quartered the agricultural landscapes of California with his mentor, Berkeley geographer Jim Parsons—without question the foremost master of California geography of the last century. For Paul, the landscapes of agricultural California are wonderlands of startling possibility: sometimes good, sometimes bad, but awaiting a producer, scholar, and any pragmatic voyager willing to travel with senses alert and eyes wide open.

Jack von Euw has for twenty years been the Curator of The Bancroft Library Pictorial Collection. In that capacity he has specialized in finding and acquiring photographers' archives from the mid twentieth century to the present. Prior to that he served as the first head of The Bancroft Library's newly formed Technical Services Unit for five years during which he established the first team dedicated to cataloging and processing pictorial materials. Jack spent his first two years at Bancroft directing digital conversion projects. And he was, before that, an archivist for the Smithsonian Institution's Archives of American Art. Jack was the lead curator for *The Bancroft Library Centennial Exhibition*, which celebrated the arrival on the Berkeley campus of the original Bancroft Collection in 1906. The exhibition contained 350 items and ran for eighteen months at the University of California Berkeley Art Museum. In addition, Jack has curated numerous exhibitions for Bancroft, including *Ansel Adams a Photographer at Work*, commemorating the 100th anniversary of Adams's birth, *California Captured on Canvas*, and co-curated *The Colors of California Agriculture*. His most recent publication is a chapter on San Francisco in the Getty Museum's 2011 Catalogue Raisonné of the Mammoth Plate Photographs of Carleton Watkins.

Food Art, Chef Tony Baker entry, Artichoke Festival

It used to be a ritual admonition delivered to children: Don't play with your food. But inventive chefs get to do just that, and the public often appreciates the humor involved. This small tableau showcases Gulliver's encounter with the Lilliputians, and was a stylish creation of Chef Tony Baker of Montrio Bistro, entered in the 2012 AGRO ART Competiton for the 53rd annual Artichoke Festival in Castroville.

Food Art, Chef Tony Baker entry, Artichoke Festival, 2012, Peter Goin.

BANC DIG 2017.14:Ag01302

Apple Blossom Lane →

MILK FARM RD 8350 →

CO___EY RD 8350 ←

DATE PALM ST

Barn Dance WY